TEAMWORK IS AN **INDIVIDUAL** SKILL

TEAMWORK
IS AN
INDIVIDUAL
SKILL

Getting Your Work Done
When Sharing Responsibility

CHRISTOPHER M. AVERY

with Meri Aaron Walker
and Erin O'Toole Murphy

BK

BERRETT-KOEHLER PUBLISHERS, INC.
San Francisco

Berrett-Koehler Publishers, Inc.
450 Sansome Street, Suite 1200
San Francisco, CA 94111-3320
Tel: (415) 288-0260   Fax: (415) 362-2512   www.bkconnection.com

ORDERING INFORMATION

Quantity sales. Special discounts are available on quantity purchases by corporations, associations, and others. For details, contact the "Special Sales Department" at the Berrett-Koehler address above.

Individual sales. Berrett-Koehler publications are available through most bookstores. They can also be ordered direct from Berrett-Koehler: Tel: (800) 929-2929; Fax: (802) 864-7626; www.bkconnection.com

Orders for college textbook/course adoption use. Please contact Berrett-Koehler: Tel: (800) 929-2929; Fax: (802) 864-7626.

Orders by U.S. trade bookstores and wholesalers. Please contact Publishers Group West, 1700 Fourth Street, Berkeley, CA 94710. Tel: (510) 528-1444; Fax (510) 528-3444.

Printed in the United States of America

Printed on acid-free and recycled paper that is composed
of 50% recovered fiber, including 10% postconsumer waste.

Library of Congress Cataloging-in-Publication Data
Avery, Christopher M., 1956–
    Teamwork is an individual skill: getting your work done when sharing responsibility/
    Christopher M. Avery with Meri Aaron Walker and Erin O'Toole Murphy.
        p. cm.
    Includes bibliographical references.
    ISBN 1-57675-155-4
    1. Teams in the workplace.   I. Walker, Meri Aaron, 1956–   II. Murphy, Erin O'Toole,
    1969–   III. Title.
HD66 .A95 2001
658.4'036—dc21   2001016141

FIRST EDITION
05   10   9   8   7   6   5

Contents

Foreword

IF YOU ARE reading this foreword in a book store, pausing for a moment after having browsed through the business management section, you are probably wondering what makes *Teamwork Is an Individual Skill* different from the other books on teamwork. Good question! The answer is that this book blends solid theory with real-world experience to create a "how-to" book from which you can start getting value immediately. That's what makes *Teamwork Is an Individual Skill* different. But there is more to the story than this . . . .

In my current role as manager of the 3M Meeting Network, I've collected a lot of data about teams and teamwork. Everything I see indicates that more and more people are doing more and more of their work as part of a team. In a 1998 survey initiated by 3M, we asked 2,800 people to profile their team-related work over the last ten years. The respondents told us that ten years ago, about 21 percent of their work was done as part of a team. When asked the same question today, those same people told us that close to 50 percent of their work is done in a team. That's a 250-percent increase over the last decade—an unprecedented change in work style.

Not only is more work being done in teams today, but there are more teams themselves. This is being driven by business trends that are happening both within and between companies. Within companies we see internal groups produced by reducing levels of management hierarchy and pushing decision making down to lower levels. We read about cross-functional and cross-organizational teams and, more recently, about downsizing, or "right-sizing" (the euphemism for doing more work with fewer people) companies. These movements cause workers to wear more hats and assume more roles. The days of one person working within the comfortable bounds of an isolated, well-defined domain is almost ancient history. We are all performing multiple roles, and we must work with other people to create a whole.

We also see increased partnering and alliances between companies. The trend toward just-in-time (JIT) manufacturing, for instance, which creates tighter supplier-manufacturer relationships and dependencies, is a good example. People are paying greater attention to supply chain management, which creates tighter interdependencies between companies that are working together to get products out the door. These factors, along with the increasing numbers of joint ventures and mergers, are all drivers of collaboration and team-related activity. Whether it occurs within companies or between companies, teaming and teamwork is the mechanism—the engine—by which work is getting done today.

My role at 3M resembles that of a circus ringmaster. What I do is keep things going in different circles around me. I keep multiple-—often unrelated—projects moving while watching for breakdowns and putting out the occasional fire. In my case, exercising teamwork as an individual skill means I have to use my personal skills to keep things moving.

Only rarely can you or I control the complement of resources available to us. And controlling other people is an illusion. So what are we left with? Our own behavior. That's it. The question then becomes: "What are the behaviors and skills we can learn and exhibit that will make our teams more likely to succeed?" This is a book about personal skills development. It's a how-to book. Christopher Avery's idea is that we can each learn how to be more effective in any work environment.

In this book Avery weaves together two different perspectives or worlds. The first world is the theoretical world of research on teamwork, group dynamics, management, and personal effectiveness.

The second world is the world of work. Christopher actually knows what people have to face every day in their work lives. He has read more about this stuff than anybody I know, and he also teaches it in his practice as an advisor to business. He has taken these concepts and academic theories and put them to the test as a trainer and a consultant. Working directly with people at the highest and lowest levels of organizations for the last decade has produced in him an insight that is in short supply in the business press. He knows from first-hand experience the problems people run into concerning team effectiveness, the expectations placed on them, and the lack of adequate resources. Christopher knows how to make these ideas about teams work for people. It's weaving together these two worlds, the academic world and the work world, that gives him a unique voice. I recommend you listen to him now.

Reading *Teamwork Is an Individual Skill* can supply the edge you need not just to survive the work week, but to thrive in it.

MICHAEL BEGEMAN, *Manager*
3M Meeting Network

Preface

IN MID-1998, I found myself at a curious place in my career as an observer of organizational behavior. Over the previous decade, my work inside some of the most successful companies in the emerging global economy had provided me a front row seat at a very interesting spectacle. As Partnerwerks associates and I worked to support the implementation and maintenance of high-performance teams in client firms, we began to witness again and again just how powerfully certain individuals' behavioral strategies impacted the effectiveness of entire teams.

Even though we were witnessing these strategies on a daily basis, we could find little written advice about how individual behavioral choices impact team effectiveness. So I began writing down some of the behaviors we were observing and every week emailing one complete principle governing the impact of behavioral choices to whomever showed interest. Soon enough, there were hundreds of subscribers to Partnerwerks' weekly tip sheet, "TeamWisdom Tips™," and more than enough essays and exercises to begin thinking about a book.

Teamwork Is an Individual Skill comes out of the first year's TeamWisdom Tips. After viewing this material I asked my associates and myself the following question: "What themes are represented here?" Five themes were identified: (1) taking personal responsibility for productive relationships, (2) creating powerful partnerships, (3) aligning individuals around a shared purpose, (4) trusting just right, and (5) developing the collaborative mindset. Each of the five main chapters of this book develops one of these themes. The chapters are ordered to provide a logical developmental path toward acquiring TeamWisdom.

These five themes make up the foundation of the text, and I see them related to each other, cognitively speaking, as a series of concentric circles. As depicted in Figure 1, "Personal Responsibility" is at the core of the skillset, with the other themes emanating outward to "Collaborative Mindset."

Figure 1. TeamWisdom Model

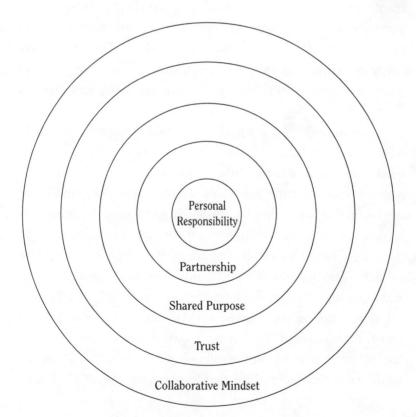

The term "TeamWisdom" contains the notion that team-work is an individual skill, not a group skill. Becoming skilled at doing more with others may be the single most important thing you can do to ensure that you remain employed in the emerging knowledge economy. This book equips you with a set of individual skills and behaviors that can and will help you create highly responsible and productive relationships at work. No longer will you find yourself complaining, "I got assigned to a bad team." Instead, you will know what to do to make teamwork work for you. This book aims to remove the ambiguity and magical thinking that exists around achieving success with teams. Most importantly, it will show you how you can build collaborations with one or more people, simply and powerfully, in any situation.

Since *Teamwork Is an Individual Skill* is designed to help you get more done with others, you can work through it by yourself, or with a group or workteam. Each of the five main chapters consists of several brief sections. Following each section is a what I call a "Personal Challenge" for individuals and a "Team Challenge" for groups. These "challenges" are questions and tasks designed to help you put into practice the ideas of the section.

For individuals, this book provides a path to upgrading your approach to work relationships. Use it to prepare for new collaborations, to take responsibility for success, to search for answers following upsets, and to read, reflect, and write about effective approaches to work relationships in general. The idea is to take a series of small and meaningful steps that will add up to noticeable improvements in relationship effectiveness making you, as an individual, more valuable to more people. The skills you learn will also make others more valuable to you. As you reflect on the Personal Challenge at the end of each section, and record your responses, your TeamWisdom will grow rapidly.

If you are using *Teamwork Is an Individual Skill* with a group, a free leaders' guide can be downloaded from www. partnerwerks.com (look for "TeamWisdom Leader's Guide"). The guide is offered to help you get the most out of these concepts in a training environment. For groups, the book provides short, specific lessons that generate a common vocabulary and a shared exploration process that will open the door to deeper team cohesion, more authentic communication, improved group creativity, more effective meetings, and far more effective group decision making. Discussing the Team Challenge at the end of each section will rapidly build clarity, motivation, common practices, overall alignment of direction and outputs, and generate potential for synergy in your team.

The Introduction further develops the main ideas of the text and describes what is at stake in the changing workplace. Chapter One examines the notion that personal responsibility is the first ingredient for producing productive relationships at work. The central position of "Personal Responsibility" in Figure 1 illustrates how your choices and actions, or inaction, can always be found as the cause of your team results.

Chapter Two, "Creating Powerful Partnerships," can help you make every relationship into a collaboration as you learn and apply key interpersonal principles used by powerful partners.

Chapter Three, "Collaborating 'on' Purpose," illustrates the mighty power of shared purpose. It provides fundamental principles and skills for aligning people to a common purpose.

In Chapter Four, "Trusting Just Right," you will explore how to trust neither too little nor too much, but "just right" at anytime with anybody. By the time you finish Chapter Four you will have learned how to tether your ability to trust others to your own behaviors, not to anyone else's.

Finally, Chapter Five, "The Collaborative Mindset," will take you well past any previous team training by pushing the boundaries of collaborative principles and actions. The purpose of Chapter Five is to stretch your mind and invite you to step up to the highest level of teamwork responsibility.

As an additional benefit to individuals and groups using this book, you are invited to accept a free subscription to Team-Wisdom Tips which is delivered to you every week by email. Just send a blank email to teamwisdom-on@partnerwerks.com or use the subscription form at www.partnerwerks.com.

I wish you a world of productive relationships!

Acknowledgments

In addition to the co-contributors named on the cover, I would not have attempted or completed this project without the talents and TeamWisdom of many other people. My life partner Amy Avery consistently demonstrated (and continues to demonstrate) incredible faith that all things will work out for us. Berrett-Koehler Senior Editor Alis Valencia and production editor Jeff Davis each provided savvy and consistent Team-Wisdom in leading us toward production. For these teammates, I remain grateful.

I am also grateful for a plethora of teachers, colleagues, and friends who have each provided me directly or indirectly with TeamWisdom lessons. Some of these people are acknowledged in the pages that follow and so many more will remain silently appreciated.

Finally, I thank Professor Larry Davis Browning of the University of Texas who introduced me to the power of Team-Wisdom 19 years ago.

December, 2000   CHRISTOPHER M. AVERY, PH.D.
Austin, Texas

Introduction: Developing TeamWisdom for Personal Success

Do you share responsibility with others to get work done but don't have authority over them (and they don't have authority over you)? If your answer to this question is "yes," like millions of other people trying to sort through the structure and dynamics of the new workplace, you can benefit immensely from the ideas and tools in this book.

Are you tired of hearing, and maybe even saying, "I got put in a bad team?" I know I am. This is the most common excuse for non-performance I hear as a business advisor, and it usually comes from highly skilled professionals! Finding oneself in a bad team is not a pleasant experience. But being in a bad team is to completely miss the point. It doesn't matter whether your team is *naturally* effective or ineffective. More and more frequently people are finding that in the new workplace they have to get their work done through a team regardless of whether that team is good, bad, or somewhere in the middle. The point here is that people need to know how to make teams work for them. This book aims to show you how.

For these and many other reasons that I will share as we go along, I firmly believe that teamwork should no longer be considered a group skill. Instead, teamwork must be considered an

1

individual skill and the responsibility of every individual in the organization. Why? Not treating teamwork as an individual skill and responsibility allows otherwise highly skilled employees to justify their non-performance by pointing fingers at others. This is an especially critical issue for highly capable professionals seeking to remain employable in the future.

So, who are these workers who share responsibility for getting results but don't have control over their colleagues? Here's my far from exhaustive list:

> ► Individual contributors who must rely on the work of others in order to get their own work done: engineers, scientists, analysts, planners, marketers, sales-people, accountants, technicians, administrators, and many others.

> ► People assigned to work in teams: developers, designers, creative people, coders, specialists, engineers, and scientists.

> ► People assigned to lead teams: program managers, product managers, project managers, team leaders, matrix managers, and technical exerts.

> ► Managers and executives who wish to empower people within and across their direct authority.

This book is for anyone who works in an environment of shared responsibility. It does not matter whether the shared responsibility occurs in a formal team, in a hierarchical environment, or as the result of a management role. It does not matter whether the shared responsibility occurs in a public, private, profit, non-profit, or large or small organization. To sum up for a moment, I don't know anyone who *doesn't* work in an environment of shared responsibility. The truth is everyone can benefit from what I call "TeamWisdom™."

What Is TeamWisdom?

TeamWisdom refers to all the individual mental skills and behaviors that lead to highly responsible and productive relationships at work. The idea is based on my definition of "team": A team is a group of individuals responding successfully to the opportunity presented by shared responsibility. Thus someone with TeamWisdom takes responsibility for ensuring that the group rises to the occasion, and in the process, makes sure his own work gets done and done well.

Why should you take personal responsibility for the performance of every team in which you serve?

You don't need me to tell you that we live and work in an age of increasing reliance on teams, partnerships, collaborations, horizontal processes, value chains, and webs and networks for getting things done. Your ability to create high quality, productive relationships is fast becoming the most important factor in getting your work done at all. It once was management's job to dole out individual work and then integrate the pieces. Now, organizations are doling out the work in larger chunks to teams and expecting the teams to divide and integrate the work in a manner that is most effective and efficient for them.

TeamWisdom Can Help You . . .
Get More Done with Less Time and Energy

I have no interest in helping you learn to be a good and compliant *team player*. I consider that term to be an insulting label that connotes someone whose primary characteristic is compliance. Instead, my interest is in helping you make maximum use of a team of which you are a member. Use the team to get your work done and get your work noticed. Instead of thinking of yourself as a component in a team, I want you instead to think of yourself as being served by the team, which is a *lever* for you and your abilities. That's right, my invitation is for you to learn to see your relationships at work as opportunities to leverage your talents and get results.

In my experience, people who approach every work relationship with the intention that they are going to take 100-percent responsibility for the quality and productivity of that relationship actually get more done with less effort.

How is getting more from less possible, you may ask? Synergy. Synergy is an overused term that few people accurately understand, but people with TeamWisdom understand it. The reason you can get more done with less time and energy is because any relationship that operates highly has far greater output than the individual input of the collaborators. This occurs because team members in high performing relationships do a much better job of applying the unique perspectives, information, and abilities that each member brings to the collaboration. Now, wouldn't you like to consistently do more with less and reap the extra rewards? I am convinced that if we all understood synergy better, we would be much happier when working interdependently because we would actually see that our reward can consistently be greater than our effort.

. . . Earn More

If you know how to produce synergy in a relationship, you can create employment situations where you are consistently producing more value. You know how to leverage your own value through a team (and you know how to leverage your teammates' value too).

I believe that we are not very far from the day when most professionals will be measured not on individual deliverables and output, but on how their teams perform and on how well they are able to get their work done.

. . . Attain Satisfaction

People who take 100-percent responsibility for creating quality, productive relationships at work tend to struggle less with bureaucracy and politics. Instead, they are more interested in getting work done. Responsible relationships invite people to use their expertise in the most efficient way possible. Such relationships reward your psyche and spirit, and allow you to make an impact and be acknowledged.

. . . Transform Your Workplace

By implementing the ideas in this book, you can help your organization and its members by helping yourself. Imagine a place where people do not blame others or make excuses when things go wrong. Imagine a place where agendas are aligned instead of hidden and where everyone can win instead of living in fear of losing. Everyday, through your own actions, you either reinforce the way things currently are or else demonstrate a different possibility and preference.

Understanding Hierarchies and Teams

Change consultants promote and build teams both as a means for achieving change and as a means for accomplishing work in changing environments. Because of their integrative nature, teams, we hold, are more flexible, innovative, permeable, responsive, and adaptive than are hierarchies. Teams also engender greater commitment from members who develop a sense of purpose and ownership by having a voice in what gets done.

But even teams can sometimes come up short.

Teaming can be really tough to get started and maintain. Many individuals—especially smart, high achievers—can experience great angst if asked to serve in teams. They can go to great lengths to avoid anything that smells like a team. Like the "starter" culture necessary for making a new batch of sourdough bread, there is a "cultural ooze" required for teamwork to flourish. This general orientation is harder to engender among certain individuals and in some organizational environments.

People blame the hierarchical culture, and I think it's true that if hierarchies did not produce the familiar controlling mindset that bogs down organizational progress, there would be no need for the teams movement. Teamwork often develops naturally and easily. Just visit any playground in the world to observe that girls and boys know innately by age five how to organize themselves around a shared task. This suggests that teamwork is a natural human process, and a skillset at least partially developed at an early age in every individual.

Are Hierarchies and Teams Compatible?

I have found that images and metaphors can help when drawing distinctions between hierarchies and teams. The purpose of the illustration below is to help you begin associating "tall" social structures with hierarchical organizations and "flat" social structures with team organizations.

Consider the image on the left in Figure I.1, "Tall Structure," to be the typical accountability hierarchy or chain

Figure I.1. Tall Organizational Structure
vs. Flat Organizational Structure

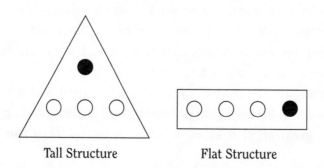

Tall Structure   Flat Structure

of command. And consider the structure on the right, "Flat Structure," to be the typical team where people share responsibility for a result but do not have authority over one another. The image on the left is likely to trigger our recollection of acts of authority, direction, delegation, accountability, evaluation, and performance management (all characteristics of traditional management that are respected because they get things done, but are criticized for being overly controlling and stodgy). The image on the right, on the other hand, is likely to trigger our recollection of opportunities for participation, more diverse perspectives, emergent roles, a clash of differences, consensus, empowerment, and informal task-focused feedback (all characteristics of what we like about teams).

Two questions come to mind: Is either organizational structure right or wrong? Does any organization exist as purely tall or purely flat?

My response is that there is good and bad in both structures. Although I am dedicated to understanding and developing team performance, I am not a hierarchy-basher at all. I find the hierarchy and its chain of command extremely useful. I also don't ever recall seeing a pure hierarchy or a pure team in a collective larger than a few individuals. Every organization is obviously a hybrid of both tall and flat structures using hierarchies for role assignments, for instance, and teams (not necessarily "formal" teams) for managing complex interdependencies.

Forming Teams in Hierarchies

Although exhibiting team skills within hierarchical organizations can be difficult, it isn't impossible. And even though individualism, competitiveness, authority and accountability systems, control, and right/wrong thinking (many of the things that have made the hierarchy and chain of command powerful) often impede the usefulness of team skill, it doesn't mean one should throw away the hierarchy as a basic organizing structure.

Many proponents of teams do eschew the hierarchy, labeling it ancient, corrupt, and wrong, but I have seen scant few large-scale team-based companies. I have seen many large hierarchical organizations in which teams can and do flourish, however. Thus I conclude that teams and hierarchies are in fact compatible and complimentary organizing systems. And hierarchical structuring is not the only reason teams fail in some organizational systems. No, I believe that the challenges are mostly attitudinal and that they manifest themselves in these forms:

▶ Avoiding responsibility (as different from a preference for individual accountability, a distinction which will be addressed below)
▶ Right/wrong thinking
▶ Win/lose thinking
▶ Carrot-or-stick thinking
▶ Skill set/role thinking

I came to this position regarding the possibility of introducing team relationships within hierarchical organizations after noticing that all relationships include collaborative and competitive forces simultaneously (we respond to whichever force is perceived as greater), and after years of observing and helping to develop collaboration under competitive conditions. I am now confident that operating successfully in teams and operating successfully in hierarchies are complimentary skill sets that already exist within most professionals.

My premise is simply this: Every individual at work can be far more productive if she will take complete responsibility for the quality and productivity of each team or relationship of which she is a part. What does this mean? In brief, it means:

▶ You may indeed have individual accountabilities, but accomplishing these will almost always depend on successful relationships with others and their work.

► You can better attend to your own accountabilities when you assume responsibility for a larger, shared task or deliverable.

► Your success depends on teams. Teamwork is an individual—not group—skill and should be treated as such.

► Individuals make a huge difference in teams, for better or worse. You can easily learn what kind of difference you make and how to build and rebuild a team.

To Take Full Advantage of TeamWisdom You Must Change Your Habits of Mind

What must change so that you can treat teamwork as an individual skill, even within a competitive hierarchical environment? The single most important thing is to understand how you can take responsibility for relationships while being accountable for deliverables at the same time. To do so start distinguishing between "accountability" and "responsibility" in the workplace.

As Figure I.2 demonstrates, accountability means to be held to account *for* something, often expressed in terms of a quality and quantity of results and stewardship of resources within a time frame, to somebody. Accountability is usually negotiated and assigned through employment agreements. Any hierarchy relies in large measure on accountability. Each person occupying a position in a hierarchy is accountable for all operations performed by the people who report to that position. The person occupying the position delegates his accountabilities (without giving up accountability) to others to perform. Each person remains accountable to whomever delegated the accountability to him.

If you work in a hierarchy and are not absolutely clear to whom you are accountable (the person who evaluates your

Figure I.2. Understanding Accountability

performance) and for what you are accountable (the quality and quantity of results), you may be in danger of never knowing whether or not your work is relevant. I suggest that you take responsibility for allowing this to happen and that you correct the situation.

Responsibility, on the other hand, means, literally, *the ability to respond.* One of the first things I ask of any group with whom I work is that each group member operate from the position of taking 100-percent personal responsibility for her own actions and results. The Responsibility Chart, Figure I.3 below, illustrates what I mean.[1] Below the center line on the chart are the terms "Lay Blame" and "Justify," two behaviors human beings engage in with amazing consistency when things don't go their way. Above the center line is an alternative. That alternative is to completely own your choices and results: "Oh, I did that. Look at my mess. Now, what can I learn from this so that I can improve and move on?" In ten years of asking thousands of individuals to operate with me above the line in seminars and in teams, no one has ever refused. Some have squirmed uncomfortably at first, but everyone has come to recognize the possibilities. Most find acting with responsibility refreshing. Some find it long overdue in their environment. Everyone finds it challenging and appreciates being in a group that will support them in learning to operate from this mindset.

Figure I.3. Responsibility Chart

```
┌─────────────────────────────────┐
│                                 │
│          RESPONSIBILITY         │
│          ───────────────        │
│                                 │
│             JUSTIFY             │
│            LAY BLAME            │
│                                 │
└─────────────────────────────────┘
```

For me, the toughest thing about taking 100-percent responsibility for my results in life, including the quality and productivity of my relationships at work, is admitting that I create my own results. If I don't like my life and results, I am the only one who can do anything about it. If I want to have a different experience, it is up to me. The tough thing about taking 100-percent responsibility is accepting that I am operating from my own agency even when I attempt to deny it, blame others, or justify my poor performance with a creative story or excuse!

When people talk of responsibility as "taking ownership," I think this is what they mean. A person who demonstrates responsibility holds an intention for overseeing the course of some process or activity (such as a shared task). Thus "responsibility" is an internal experience. It is an urge, feeling, or mindset that facilitates the bringing about of some result.

While responsibility is an internal quality, accountability is an external one. To say it another way, accountability can be assigned, but responsibility can only be taken.

Accountability and responsibility are not mutually exclusive. In fact, they are extremely complimentary. It is time for each of us in the workplace to take responsibility for relationships as well as accountability for deliverables, and to engage in the conversations that build productive relationships at work. As Figure I.4 demonstrates sharing responsibility means recognizing and working to optimize your interdependence with all your work partners. That is, there are actions you can take to improve their results and yours.

Figure I.4. Sharing Responsibility

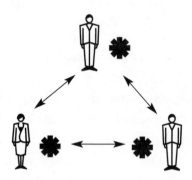

Amazing things happen when two or more people commit themselves to operating from a position of responsibility: Mistakes are viewed as opportunities to learn; communication approaches authentic completeness; and learning and progress happen fast. And all it takes for a group to operate from responsibility is for one member of that group to demonstrate responsibility and request it of the others.

To help you get the most out of this book, I will be that one individual, and here comes my request. As you consider the ideas that follow, ask yourself if you are willing to do your best to live the rest of your life "above the line."

Accept Accountability for Deliverables and Take Responsibility for Relationships

The first change we can make is the way we look at our roles in organizational life. In our organizations, we divide up large tasks into smaller tasks and distribute those smaller tasks to individuals. Whether manager or individual contributor, employee or contractor, exempt or non-exempt, we are all accustomed to taking accountability for deliverables.

People with TeamWisdom however go a step further. They back away from their task, role, and deliverables to view the interdependencies upstream, downstream, and all around them. Then they commit to taking responsibility for the quality and productivity of these relationships that will help them meet their accountabilities.

What do you have to do to develop your own TeamWisdom? The next step is to recognize and decide that you can't change anyone other than yourself. Got that? The only person that you can change is yourself. If you want things around you to change, first you must change. If you are willing to adopt that stance, you are ready to consider how to take responsibility when you do not have authority.

Responsibility without Authority

The message of this book is that your workteams and other work relationships will increase your personal productivity to the highest level possible only if you are willing to take 100-percent responsibility for the quality of each team or relationship, regardless of who has authority.

People in organizations frequently balk at taking responsibility without authority. We desire the authority to distribute and delegate tasks and deliverables to others, and we certainly don't want to depend on anyone else's performance for our rewards! Authority, we believe, is power, and the ability to get things done. But authority is not the only source of power, and there are better ways to get things done.

The most important teambuilding principle that I know, which I write about at length in this book, contradicts the notion that authority is the best way to get things done. The most important teambuilding principle I know is: *The task is the reason for the team.* What this means is that teams are defined not by the people on them but by what the team must do. A teambuilder with TeamWisdom applies this principle in the process of constructing a team by figuring out how to organize the work so that none of the members can win individually but rather must win first as a team. This is a powerful way to get your work done. I call it "power with" and note that it is quite different from "power over" authority.

In summary, what needs to change for you to build Team-Wisdom is the habit of mind that denies personal responsibility. You must be willing to own results that are larger than yourself. You must be willing to work interdependently with others. True collective leverage and power comes not from distributing and delegating accountabilities, but from collectively demonstrating responsibility for the entire result while doing your best to make your contribution useful to others.

How Do You Get Things Done without Control?

Teambuilding is simply a set of messages successfully shared among a group of people. Any individual can easily learn and practice teambuilding if she chooses. Professionals often use challenge courses, personality inventories, and other games and exercises to provoke groups into sharing this set of messages. But when such tools are used without understanding exactly why, critical communication skills can become hidden and results can appear magical. Individuals who want to get their work done through interaction with others must learn to make their wants and desires known without ambiguity and without magical thinking. To maximize team performance I recommend that team members engage in the following five conversations as the first order of business after the team has been formed:

Conversation One: Focusing on the Collective Task

If you are assigned to a team, or just want to create a team atmosphere at work, the first thing you should do is establish shared clarity about what the team was formed to do. Team-building starts with clarifying the reason for the team. It does not start with getting people to like each other better. The task itself, not the people performing the task, is the reason for the team. This is why Tom Peters' new passion for the phrase "project focus" is right on target.[2] What Peters means by "project focus" (and what I mean by "task") is that when work has specific beginnings, ends, deliverables, and results, people can get more focused on it. By the nature of its task focus, then, a team is temporary because that task has a beginning and an end.

Thirty years ago the academic literature describing the concept of group cohesion focused on how much group members liked each other. Today, however, the literature points more to shared interest in a common result as the best predictor of group cohesion. So the first conversation for any new team should be how to work together to accomplish something larger than any one member of the team. If you think about it, you will understand that the move from independence to interdependence begins with asking for or giving help. You will find plenty of practical advice in the following chapters on how to do that.

Conversation Two: Aligning Interests

The second conversation to have concerns members' individual reasons for contributing to the collective task (remember that commitment to other members is a by-product of having an individual stake in the collective outcome). Making sure everyone is at the same level of motivation is far more important to successful teamwork than matching appropriate skills.

Skill mix is an important issue for project management, but it isn't necessary for teamwork. Why? If members don't have the required skills, a high performance team will improvise. The same is not true for motivation, however. Every team performs to the level of its least invested member. Always. I call this "the principle of the least invested coworker." Because this principle of group behavior is not widely taught, most team members don't know how to respond when it manifests itself, and it manifests itself frequently. I figure "the principle of the least invested coworker" costs billions of dollars annually in lost productivity.

People do recognize one element of the principle, however, and that is freeloading: individuals who don't do their part. Freeloaders are actually an invention of institutions. Naturally forming teams don't have them; freeloaders only show up in institutionally sanctioned teams with assigned members. If not for the bureaucracy protecting each freeloader's membership, the team would unload him immediately if he didn't quit on his own first.

Most professionals aren't equipped to align motivations or confront freeloaders, but it isn't difficult to do. It isn't so much a lack of skill as a lack of perceived permission and responsibility. The most common excuse I hear for not addressing issues of low motivation and commitment on teams is "that's management's job." You can make it your job if you want to get more done. This book will show you how.

Conversation Three: Establishing Behavioral Ground Rules

The widely used four-phase model of team formation (forming, storming, norming, and performing), suggests that norms don't develop until phase three. You can accelerate the development of norms, however, by initiating a conversation about appropriate and inappropriate behavior in your collective effort and then enforcing those agreements.

Turn back to page 6 and look again at Figure I.1. Notice that the image on the left, the tall structure, is rife with assumptions about who can decide direction, who can judge, how communication and feedback will flow, who can and can't evaluate work, etc. That's the tremendous power of the hierarchy. The image on the right, the flat structure, has far fewer such inherent relationship guidelines (which gives it its unique power!). The third critical teambuilding conversation then focuses on how members should treat each other when working together in the team.

Whatever operating agreements are made must be policed by the team. Team members must be equipped to "call" each other on broken agreements the way baseball umpires call each batted ball fair or foul. Until employees learn the distinction between tall and flat organizational structures, and how it is in their individual and collective interest to provide behavioral feedback to teammates, most won't "call" teammates on behavioral issues. They won't because most of them believe "It's management's job." But you can make it your job.

Conversation Four: Setting Bold Goals and Anticipating Conflicts, Breakthroughs, and Synergy

Unless they have experienced it a number of times, few employees appreciate and anticipate how their work on a team can lead to real breakthroughs. This lack of understanding contributes to resistance toward team activities. The fourth conversation you must have with colleagues at the beginning of team formation then is about setting bold goals, the anticipation of conflicts in working toward such goals, breakthroughs, and synergy.

When it comes to productivity, team performance corresponds to the first-half of the classic S-curve. Due to the team's flat organizational structure (shared responsibility without authority), members require time to orient themselves to each other and to the task. Thus, performance is frequently flat for the first half of the team's investment of time and energy (see Figure I.5). After this initial period, however, breakthroughs will occur and the team's performance turns up rapidly. If you understand this pattern, you can anticipate it. The "high performance" part of teamwork is always temporary, not sustained. Teams, unlike in-stitutionalized departments, do have beginnings and ends as their collective tasks begin and end and the high performance part of the cycle is at the end.

Figure I.5. Productivity on a High Performance Team

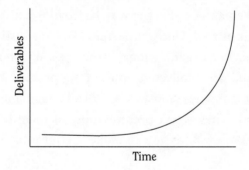

Conversation Five: Honoring Individuals and Their Differences

Differences in perspectives are powerful, especially when they are aimed at a collective task in an environment of trust. Team members must create explicit opportunities for each team member to participate and add value. The goal is to produce synergy through the discussion and appreciation of different perspectives. Two types of behavior kill synergy: people saying more than they know, and people saying less than they know. The fifth conversation, then, should be designed to discover what each member brings to the task and to honor differences in perspective and approach. From this utilitarian viewpoint, diversity is not about morality. It's not even about equal opportunity as an end in itself. Diversity is about productivity, breakthrough, and synergy.

Individual contributors must learn how to stay engaged with each other under time and performance pressures. They must expect that their interactions will lead to breakthroughs that create results beyond their imaginings. More importantly, individuals must learn how to talk about these dynamic relationships in ways that create breakthroughs rather than breakdowns.

Playing a Win/Win Game in a Win/Lose World

The most compelling reason to acquire TeamWisdom skills, and my primary motivation for writing this book, is my own desire, which I have come to discover that I share with millions of other professionals, to play a win/win game at work. In my experience, it isn't teamwork that is difficult. It's initiating teamwork in a world of business that is antagonistic toward teamwork. The issue that must be addressed is that we are trying to perform teamwork within and between hierarchical organizations where a predominant feature is competitiveness—if not outright antagonism—and where win/lose intentions and results are the norm. Teamwork would be easy without the sometimes contradictory demands of the hierarchical chain of command, the politics and the bureaucracy. The issue for many in the new workplace, then, is learning how to cooperate under competitive conditions. The central question is: "How do I play win/win in a seemingly win/lose world?"

Our Metaphors Are Slow to Change

Think about this. People in organizations have been using and studying hierarchy as an organizing principle for a long,

long time. The Roman Catholic Church and the Roman Army used hierarchy to organize and manage large numbers of individual members spread out over vast areas, and studies of hierarchical organization date back to this time. The Catholic Church thrives in much the same organizational form that it has used for hundreds and hundreds of years.

Organization managers and scientists have only been exploring the use of teams for about 50 years. And it's only been 20 years since people noticed that the U.S. economy was taking a beating and began examining Japanese management techniques. When I was a new doctoral student at The University of Texas at Austin in 1982, I discovered the first three books to appear in university libraries about teams in Japan. I used them to design Quality Circle teams and team training for a Motorola facility in Austin. Those books were brand new then. The hundreds, perhaps thousands, of books about teams that you can buy today have all been written in the last 20 years.

It is interesting to watch what typically happens when a traditional organization experiments with teams. First, a big hurrah will be sounded: "We are going to teams!" Then, people get reorganized into new accountability hierarchies that look just like the old ones, except that the new ones have different labels. The team (former department) is assigned a leader (former manager). The leader is assigned the accountability. The team members (former subordinates) wait for the leader to tell them what to do so they can each do their part.

The labels may have changed, but the organizing metaphor hasn't changed at all. And I have seen this same process repeated hundreds of times. But it isn't a conscious conspiracy to keep things from changing. Managers initiate this kind of false change because they don't know any other way. They don't know what they don't know. So they re-structure and change the words, not recognizing that they are actually recreating what they say they are trying to change.

Think about it. Our images and metaphors of organization are all about authority and chain of command. TeamWisdom seeks out new metaphors.

Tired Ideas about Teambuilding

I am very concerned about the nature of teambuilding and the role of teambuilding consultants in industry. Let me conclude this introduction by briefly addressing some common practices that I find troubling.

In the table below, the left column contains the common understanding, or what I would call "mythology," about teams and teambuilding. The right column contains my experience of the same subject, which tends to deflate the myth.

Common Teambuilding Myths	My Experience
Teambuilding is treated by both providers and consumers as *bonding magic;* an art rather than a science, understood only by consultants who must be brought in from the outside.	Teambuilding is a series of specific communications or conversations that occur between people who could share responsibility to get something done. Anyone can have these conversations with coworkers.
If we are doing teambuilding, we aren't getting real work done. Doing teambuilding means taking time out from the real work.	Teambuilding happens in the course of work. If it doesn't happen naturally (as is frequently the case), then there are a series of conversations that people can invoke about their work in order to build the team.
The first step in teambuilding is for people to appreciate each other more (personality inventories are important to building the team).	Teams can perform well even when members don't like each other. When teams form naturally, the most likely first step is understanding what the team has been established to do, i.e., clarifying shared responsibility.

Common Teambuilding Myths	My Experience
Teams *get built* (by someone) and stay that way. A common variation of this myth is that the time to do teambuilding is when relationships are in high conflict.	Teams don't stay built. Many events can occur during the life of a team to break the team's healthy dynamics. An organization shouldn't depend on outside consultants to make teams happen. A better solution is for professionals who work in shared responsibility environments to learn how to build teams for themselves.

What I propose in this book is preposterous to many people. The very idea that we should think of teamwork as an individual responsibility and an individual skill set violates decades of teaching about teams. It's an idea that is easy to dismiss because it sounds so absurd. It sounds absurd for this reason: As workers, we hold a deeply imbedded belief that we are supposed to do only our part. We aren't supposed to take responsibility for the whole team being successful. "That's not fair!" we say.

I, of course, maintain that you should take responsibility for the whole team being successful. If this sounds absurd, so be it. I have to admit that I am somewhat attracted by the absurdity. With the TeamWisdom skills you will learn in this book, you can be absurd yourself and make a difference in the way you approach your work. You can make yourself invaluable to your organization no matter what your technical expertise, and you can use teams to get your own work done.

1

Teamwork As an Individual–Not Group–Skill

TEAMWISDOM INVITATION

When I close my eyes and imagine a workplace in which all employees are totally responsible for their team experiences and results, I see several conditions that have made this possible:

▸ Teams have the power to select their own members.

▸ Everyone clearly understands team goals and feels personally responsible for attaining them.

▸ Expectations of performance and contributions of team members have been made explicit.

▸ Team members expect to give and receive regular feedback from each other and, thereby, hold each other to agreed upon standards.

▸ Rewards and recognition are based on team results.

To create and sustain this kind of workplace—not just in the imagination but in everyday experience—requires each of us to take personal responsibility for the ways we participate in teams. While this sounds simple enough, it is much easier to say than to do. Otherwise, I wouldn't have to close my eyes to imagine such a place. Despite their differences, I think most people actively desire to work in these kinds of teams. We all value clarity, reciprocity, and interdependence. The problem is not all of us know how to create and maintain the circumstances that support them.

For example, my company's executive team recently was defining our business strategy for the year with the help of an outside consultant. As we debated how best to prioritize approaches to growing our subscriber base, most people said our top priority should be pursuing new customer segments. I took the position that our first priority should be retaining current customers, then adding new customers on top of the existing base. Although this position was initially put down, I stuck with it. Little by little, other members of the team began to incorporate customer retention into their push for growth, and our final approach was richer, broader, and deeper because of my willingness to stand by a less than popular opinion.

By learning to apply the tools and principles explored in this book, each of us can increase our personal power and responsibility on workteams. The context we establish won't be conflict-free. It will be dynamic, creative, and collaborative. Instead of suppressing our disagreement with a prevailing opinion, we will contribute regularly, responsibly, and with respect for other points of view.

SUSAN INGRAHAM ASHLEY
Vice President, Human Resources
Houston Cellular Telephone Company

What Is "TeamWisdom?"

If you know your behavior will make a difference in the
success of a team, you may already have TeamWisdom.
If you don't, develop it!

Remember the last time you noticed something for the first time
and then started seeing it pop up everywhere? Sometimes it
happens with a make of car, a hairstyle, or a song on the radio.
For me, it happened as a result of my observation of team skills
in professional environments. A few years ago, I began noticing
smart and otherwise highly skilled professionals demonstrating
and espousing the following beliefs—which I see as myths—
about teams:

▶ Myth #1: Since teamwork is a group experience,
  individuals can't be responsible for the quality of
  their team efforts.

▶ Myth #2: Getting in a good team is mostly a matter
  of luck.

▶ Myth #3: If you are in a poorly functioning team,
  and are not in charge, there is little you can do but
  grin and bear it.

Despite massive research and reporting to the contrary,
these myths remain rampant among intelligent professionals.
And they exact an enormous toll in lost productivity and low
morale among individuals, teams, and whole organizations.

As I have come to see it, the truth is very different. Many
people demonstrate another set of beliefs and skills about teamwork. And they are generally the most successful people in all
environments. My associates and I have made it our business to
identify, watch, and learn from these people. And we have
adopted "TeamWisdom" as the name for the plexus of skills
and behaviors these people demonstrate.

Contradicting the myths above, people with TeamWisdom:

▶ Understand and act on all of their personal abilities to affect their entire team's effectiveness.

▶ Know that being in a good team isn't random. Instead, it is a function of one's relationship behavior and what you and others do.

▶ Take personal responsibility for the quality of their relationships. They never wait for those "in charge" to notice and act on a situation that needs attention.

In a nutshell, TeamWisdom is a specific set of attitudes and behaviors that make "teamwork" an individual skill, not some elusive outcome of group dynamics available only by the luck of the draw. TeamWisdom is something that every one of us can grow for ourselves, no matter what position we play in a team.

Personal Challenge

Consider your most recent team experiences. Playback your internal conversation about those teams and listen for your beliefs about your experiences. Based on the three criteria above, would you give yourself a high rating for TeamWisdom? What would have to change for your TeamWisdom rating to increase? Be specific. What can you do to cause this change to happen?

Team Challenge

Discuss with your team how the quality of individuals' participation effects the quality of the team's results. In what specific ways can your team support the participation of all members and their development of TeamWisdom? Record your responses in a shared space and refer to them daily over the coming week.

TeamWisdom Applied

An Executive with Superior TeamWisdom

Herb Kelleher of Southwest Airlines is a CEO who exhibits extraordinary TeamWisdom. Kelleher has led the most profitable airline in the country in recent years, and he tolerates no business solutions that don't completely honor both customers and employees.

For example, Southwest executives enjoy many of the usual perks of executive status. However, they are also required to report to work on the busiest travel days of the year, which often occur on holidays and weekends. On these days, instead of reporting to their offices, Southwest executives back up baggage handlers and gate agents!

Think of the message it sends across the company that on the most backbreaking days of the year, the company's top officers can be counted in the trenches, working side-by-side with the baggage handlers. That's TeamWisdom!

Teamwork As an Individual Event

Raise your standards for good team performance, and start being responsible for your own team experience.

Most people go from project to project doing little more than hoping this team will provide them with a good experience. What's the result? An overwhelming majority of professionals have learned to expect a mediocre team experience, not a great one.

You may know the routine: You join a new team hoping that this time team members will finally act like a team. When they don't, you lower your hopes, your standards, and maybe even your commitment. Then you worry about your individual performance appraisal and may resent that you are assigned to teams.

What's the alternative? Stop operating on hope and start operating on intention and knowledge. Raise your standards for, and commitment to, great team performance. How? Forget the popular phrase "There is no 'I' in team." There is too, and it's you! To make teamwork an individual event, start taking total responsibility for your own team experience. To do that:

▸ Recognize that you are not a passive recipient in teams, that your behavior shapes every team you serve, and that you affect the team at least as much as it affects you.

▸ Acknowledge that *not* attending to team performance *is* a choice and that you are choosing to put yourself at the mercy of chance.

▸ Accept that if you are in a situation of shared responsibility and/or shared reward, then the quality and productivity of the relationships are worthy of your focus.

▸ Learn what behaviors and processes lead to successful teams and exhibit them.

Personal Challenge

Ask yourself what it means to be "totally responsible" for your own team experience. How does taking total responsibility change your attitude and behavior as a team member?

Team Challenge

Discuss with your team what kind of team experience you want to have together. What would a great team experience look like for each one of you?

TeamWisdom Applied

One Member Provides Structure for the Team

Harold sat in the meeting on Saturday morning wishing he were on the golf course. It was a meeting among four principals of a consulting firm plus Harold, a marketing consultant. After about 45 minutes of circular conversation that revealed more about the political dynamics among the four principals than about the content of the meeting, the CEO turned to Harold—who hadn't yet spoken—and asked what he thought. Harold's response was enlightening. He said "I want to be helpful, and I'm not exactly clear what we are trying to do here this morning" then looked at the CEO inviting his response. The CEO explained the morning's task from his point of view. Then Harold asked each of the other principals in turn to articulate what they thought the group was there to do that morning. When Harold was satisfied that they all shared the same purpose, he turned back to the CEO and asked "what's in it for you to take your Saturday morning to do that?" The CEO and each principal responded in turn revealing their interests and verbalizing their commitment. After that, Harold asked a few more questions of each person, questions like "Are there any ground rules that I should be aware of here?" and

"What do you bring to this task?" He then stood at a flip chart and said "Now that we are all on the same page together, tell me what steps we have to take to achieve our purpose here this morning." The team was tight, energized, on task, and finished in time for Harold to get to the golf course.

Agree to Response-Ability

When you choose to respond intentionally to whatever happens in life, you have the key to personal power and growth.

Have you noticed that people who face what they don't like about their lives with denial, blame, or justification get to keep things that way? Such people assign the cause of their problems to others. By saying "It's not my fault," they box themselves in. Many conflicts at work are caused by two people, departments, or organizations seeing the other party as the cause of their misery with no way out. The reward for this choice of behavior is that they get to stay in their misery!

I prefer to team with people who believe that they create all of their life's results—good and bad, big and small. With such a belief, there is only one person who can change what isn't working—oneself. The difference is a simple switch of mindset: Agree to internalize the cause of your results ("I did this to me") rather than externalize ("They/It did this to me"). From that position, you need not stay in any undesirable condition.

When we adopt this switch, we become more willing and able to respond to life (and team) situations. Becoming consistently more willing and able to respond (response-ability) to whatever happens in your life and work is the key to personal power and growth. It's also the key to productive relationships.

So, when I find myself in a non-productive or counter-productive relationship, rather than deny, blame, or justify, I am likely to ask myself, "How did I create this for myself? And now, how will I respond to change it?"

Personal Challenge

Examine your life and work while asking yourself if it's possible that every result you experience is of your own creation. Then immediately answer, "Yes," and determine how this is true.

Team Challenge

Discuss with your teammates what happened when your team avoided taking responsibility for negative results by denying, laying blame, or justifying? How can you agree to take full responsibility for your results?

TeamWisdom Applied

A Manager Who Took Response-Ability

During an annual account review, a Ford executive announced to his Motorola counterparts that Ford wasn't nearly as pleased with Motorola's performance that year as Motorola had announced it was. Ford went on to list 19 specific dissatisfactions with Motorola's service concerning that year's $60 million purchase of Motorola computer chips for Ford car engines. One of the most stinging complaints was "lack of executive commitment."

To demonstrate his executive commitment, Motorola corporate vice-president Gary Johnson assembled a cross-functional team, which promptly launched a blame-storm on Ford's list of dissatisfactions. By the group's third meeting, Johnson began to see a better approach. He asked the group to read the list of dissatisfactions as

Ford's "menu for happiness." Instead of spending any further time refuting the validity of the claims, Johnson invited the team to accept them as fact and to address them from Ford's—not Motorola's—point of view.

The team began applying Ford's standards instead of Motorola's internal measurement devices to Motorola's manufacturing and delivery processes and, within a year, stabilized the account. Under two years after the list of dissatisfactions was issued, Motorola won Ford's highest supplier quality rating. After three years, Ford awarded Motorola an additional $250 million worth of business that had previously gone to Motorola's arch-rival. That's the power of taking response-ability.

Is Your Silence Consent?

Treat every action and decision in a relationship as one you "consent to." Or decline the relationship.

At one time, I was presented an opportunity to accept a new business relationship. As I listened to my internal dialogue about the proposition, I noticed I kept coming back to my fundamental belief that teamwork is an individual (not a group) skill and responsibility. Only I am responsible for the quality of all my work relationships.

What does this have to do with my decision-making process? Or with yours, when you are asked to join a team? Well, if teamwork is an individual skill, then when we elect to become part of a team:

▶ We retain our personal power.

▶ We lend our consent to a group direction and purpose.

▶ We incur a responsibility to speak up when we disagree with the group's direction or purpose.

Said another way, people with true TeamWisdom act *as if* they are always building consensus, even if the team relationship is based on authority, majority, or some other form of governance. They empower, approve of, and cooperate with a wide variety of group decisions aimed at achieving an agreed direction and purpose. People with true TeamWisdom don't find it necessary to voice an opinion on every detail. They just focus on purpose, direction, and values and let the rest go. Or, they decline the relationship.

Contrary to the popular definition, real "team players" never "go along" with something about which they have strong negative feelings. They retain and exercise their personal power at all times. They remain conscious that authority relationships are just agreements—consents—between people. When true teammates disagree with teammates, partners, bosses, or elected representatives, they push back, knowing that the group's final direction will either represent their personal consent to that direction or represent the place where they withdraw from the group.

"Going along" without passion or commitment creates two phenomena:

▶ Entire groups going where no member wants to go.[1]

▶ People hanging out together with low commitment, low energy, low performance, resentment, and low esteem.

In my personal situation, I eventually saw that I lacked sufficient passion for the work to participate patiently in the group's process. Since my predisposition was to change the group's direction, without serious passion to fuel my efforts, I was better off not becoming a member. And the group was better off, too.

Personal Challenge

Consider the truth in this statement: No decision or action that affects you can be made without your consent (even if registered by your silent tolerance or permission). If this confuses you, or you balk at the thought, please just stay open to the idea and consider how it might be possible. As you reflect, make note of how you feel about past teamwork and your desire to speak your mind.

Team Challenge

Discuss with each other the ways in which consent shows up in your team. What new agreements would help support healthy behaviors regarding members' consent to team actions, decisions, and processes?

TeamWisdom Quoted

"Companies tend to be allergic to conflict—particularly companies that have been in operation for a long time. Being averse to conflict is understandable. Conflict is dangerous. It can damage relationships. It can threaten friendships. But conflict is the primary engine of creativity and innovation."

Ronald Hiefetz, Director of the Leadership
Education Project, Harvard University[2]

The Benefit of Showing You Can Be Provoked

Being provocable better supports responsible collaboration than "being nice."

Although "calling" others on broken agreements is critical to building trust with teammates, it can be exceedingly difficult to do. Why? Well, many of us have one or more emotional blocks to confronting others about irresponsible behavior. Let's look at what makes it seem easier to "hold the bag" than to confront others when they let us down.

We have all been in dozens of situations where coworkers' behavior appeared irresponsible, in direct violation of a promise, or damaging to productivity. It hurts. So, why in the world do we tolerate it? In my experience, there are two very good reasons why we tolerate it: We have a need to be nice, or we have an addiction to criticism.

Needing to be nice is addressed here. The next chapter addresses the addiction to criticism.

Needing to be nice—or needing to be seen as being nice—is evidence we need social approval more than we need inner congruence. Social approval is great to have. We all need and enjoy it. But, as health professionals will tell you, when social approval conflicts with personal experience, it actually can become destructive. It's called lying.

To overcome this block, we can reduce our willingness to tolerate irresponsible behavior and increase our "provocability"— that is, our ability to show what really happens inside when others' behavior hurts us. When we choose to show our true response to irresponsibility, we actually foster true collaboration with others. How? Because provocability signals integrity. And it's integrity that builds trust between coworkers.

Provocability is part of a collaborative communication strategy called "tit-for-tat." To play tit-for-tat, start interactions with cooperative behavior and, after that, match others' behavior. If they cooperate, then you cooperate. If they are uncooperative, then show provocability. Point out their uncooperative behavior and let them know you hold them responsible for the relationship: They can have it be cooperative or uncooperative.

It's up to them. Then match their moves. When used proactively, tit-for-tat is a great strategy for teaching others how to cooperate with you.

Personal Challenge

Provocability is best learned by addressing small irritations first. They are easier to confront. This week, pay conscious attention to when a coworker's behavior bugs you slightly. (*Hint:* When you are "bugged," you are provoked—that is, the other person's behavior is in some way unproductive or uncooperative in relation to you.) Show an appropriate level of provocability by identifying their behavior to them and letting them know what behavior you would prefer.

Remember, if you have been tolerating a particular behavior for some time, a relationship pattern has been set and your demonstration of provocability can be seen as "over the top." Start small and easy, then build.

Team Challenge

Discuss with your teammates the kinds of situations in which the team's tolerance of a certain unacceptable behavior is no longer productive. What team agreements can you make that will support appropriate provocability—and responsible collaborations—among team members?

TeamWisdom Applied

Giving Voice to Dissent

A 40-member software design group had agreed to use a "thumbs-up/thumbs-down" system in an all-hands meeting to achieve consensus on an important operations decision. When Jeff proposed a popular solution, 39 thumbs pointed up in support. Julie's thumb pointed down.

Under consensus rules, every member enjoys veto power but is also responsible for moving the group forward to a solution. Julie was given the floor and bravely registered a point of view that resonated within everyone. When the team polled again, many changed their votes from thumbs-up to thumbs-down and Julie became hero of the day for thinking and speaking what others felt but didn't express.

Experience Judgments Completely So You Can Clear Them Away

Identify and clear your mind of judgments, so you
can respond from choice, rather than from auto-pilot.

To prevent ourselves from spewing unnecessary judgments in productive relationships, traditional wisdom admonishes us to "judge not." But not judging is an improbable—if not impossible—action for all but the most emotionally and spiritually developed of us. So it's my practice to experience and express judgment fully, and then let it go.

Here is an example from my own experience. I recently trusted too much and found myself "holding the bag." My first reaction was to get a little peeved. Then I remembered that the bag I was holding was evidence that I trusted too much rather than too little. But I trusted! Then I congratulated myself. (I know this sounds a little silly, but who deserves our own acknowledgment more than we do?) I knew my own feedback might be the best feedback I would get in this situation. I felt better and was in a little more understanding frame of mind. Then, one-by-one, I ran a complete audit of my emotions.

Upsets are opportunities to learn. But to benefit from upsets, we have to exercise our emotional intelligence with vigor. It's our emotional intelligence that enables us to make distinctions around emotions and choose our responses. To make distinctions around emotions, we first have to examine them.

The first emotion I identified was anger. I replayed the situation that caused me to be angry until I understood it, exploring it completely. I felt I didn't deserve to be treated this way. And, I probably didn't. But so what? Then I saw that I wanted to get even (and it's important to remember that getting even is a form of "laying blame"). Since it would not serve either party for me to escalate, I decided the best approach to my anger was forgiveness.

Who needed to be forgiven? Well, the embarrassing truth was that I needed to forgive myself. Once I completely sensed my embarrassment (that is, my own blaming of myself for making a "mistake"), my first reaction was to protect myself from looking bad by installing a mental rule to never do that again. But installing mental rules (and other such attempts to operate on auto-pilot) only reduces our ability to respond, creating inflexibility rather than response-ability. Instead, I searched for the humor in the situation. Humor is a good response to embarrassment.

In this instance, I also experienced a sense of unfairness that I felt powerless to correct. My assumption was that I had to "tolerate" this person because of who he was in relation to me. (Fill in your own distinctions: better, stronger, boss, customer, teacher, coach, authority, parent, etc.) But, tolerating anything is always a choice, a personal choice. And I have learned the hard way it's a choice that often turns out poorly. Tolerating unacceptable behavior only creates resentment, which further reduces one's ability to respond.

So, once I had audited my feelings and really felt their consequences, it was actually a short step to clear the judgments. I decided I wanted to correct this relationship, so I didn't perpetuate those feelings. Since there are only three things we can do in situations we don't like—live with them, get out of them, or change them—I decided it was time for me to respond in a way that would improve the relationship.

What you say and do when you are left "holding the bag" is up to you. But remember, your actual choices are to live with the relationship, get out of it, or change it.

Personal Challenge

When your next upset occurs and you are tempted to make a quick judgment, stop. Then, with some imaginary popcorn and your favorite imaginary beverage, set up a reverse movie theater in your mind and view your emotions completely. Make sure your imaginary theater experience is fully sensory, complete with sight, sound, smell, and touch. Then, instead of making someone else the "antagonist," have yourself play all roles (hero, villain, etc.) and see what distinctions you can make.

Team Challenge

Take 20 minutes together to reflect on your recent team interactions. What criticisms have been shared (criticism always contains some negative evaluation or invalidation of the individual)? What were the responses? What could have been done differently?

TeamWisdom Quoted

"When I experience upset, the first thing I do is reground myself. My conditioned tendency for responding to bad situations is to tighten in my gut and my chest—sealing off my power and my heart—and get up in my head becoming logical and rational. Though

this allows me to move quickly, it also makes me cold, uncaring and mechanistic. Regrounding brings me back to my humanity. To do this, I check in on what emotions I am experiencing and look for a message in these feelings. Then I look back at the world with curiosity asking myself how I wish to respond to this situation. This is a position of personal power, very responsive rather than reactive. I find that, though this whole process takes less than a second, my decision making and my learning are substantially enhanced."

Ed Perry, President and CEO, Human Code

An Upset Is an Opportunity to Learn

Operate from personal responsibility,
and you will learn from every upset.

Blast yourself and your team out of "Excuse-Mentality." When things go wrong, our common response is to get upset "at" someone or something. We blame. Then we get mad. Sometimes we even feel a need to get even. Then we get mad at ourselves. Then, to be sure the situation never happens again, we make up new rules. For instance, we say things like "I will never again . . .":

- ▶ Work for a male/female manager

- ▶ Date a salesperson

- ▶ Have a business partner

- ▶ Start my own business

Unfortunately, an Excuse-Mentality doesn't free us from uncomfortable situations. In fact, assigning blame and/or making excuses may actually bind us more tightly than ever to dilemmas. It's only when we operate from a "Responsibility-Mentality" that upsets can become opportunities to learn and, potentially, to escape this and future dilemmas.

Think about it. When things don't go well, taking responsibility is actually the best way to claim the full value of a negative experience. It's only when we move from Excuse-Mentality to Responsibility-Mentality that we become ready to ask, "What can I learn from this?" Or, when we're really brave, "How did I create this?" These are the questions that harvest value from an upset. My biggest breakthroughs have come from my biggest messes and upsets. But the breakthroughs didn't show up until after I owned the mess and determined how I contributed to creating it.

From where I stand it looks like the fastest route to living freer, happier, more fulfilled lives is to adopt the Responsibility-Mentality as soon as possible. When we become upset "at" a partner, no matter what he did wrong, we will reap the greatest value from the experience when we are ready to look at how we contributed to the upset we're feeling. It's just a short step from there to seeing that the fastest way to build and maintain a learning team is to help all our teammates turn their upsets into opportunities to learn.

Personal Challenge

Choose a current aspect of your life where you are upset "at" someone or something or upset "with" a situation. Ask yourself how your own choices and actions actually created the upset. Stay with this question until you are satisfied with the answers you receive. This can be both a humbling and an immensely freeing exercise.

Team Challenge

When you catch yourself feeling upset at or with a team-mate this week, take 15 minutes to examine your own choices. Then write in a journal about how you could change your be-havior to strengthen the relationship. You may or may not need to ask for new agreements with your partners. If you see you do need new agreements, make them then and there.

TeamWisdom Applied

A Team That Learned from Being Upset

Under immense pressure, a Wells Fargo business devel-opment team produced a new, online banking business. During the development process, team members suffered repeated experiences of frustration. The team decided to introduce a tool that would enable the group to benefit from upsets as they were encountered.

Every time the team got stuck as a group, or, when one or more members acted out in frustration, some member would "call it." In other words, she would an-nounce, "Let's clear this, so we can get past it." Then, instead of shoving the upset aside to fester, the group would immediately explore the assumptions that had been made by individuals or the team as a whole that might have fueled the upset. As erroneous assumptions were uncovered and cleared up, the group benefited from additional information and found important new directions to pursue.

Conceive New Relationships as Avenues of Contribution

In new relationships, ask yourself what you can do to facilitate collaboration. Then do it!

Observing diplomats, international delegations, ambassadors, and other dignitaries from other countries can teach us important lessons in TeamWisdom. When one dignitary visits another, they arrive bearing gifts. And what do the gifts symbolize? Our contemporary cynicism can tempt us to see them as "bribes," but this isn't wholly fair.

First, such gifts celebrate a new and promising relationship. They also symbolize a willingness on the part of the giver to invest first and look for the payoff later. Quite often, gifts indicate a real—rather than symbolic—contribution that one party brings to the new relationship. The real contribution could be a treaty, an investment, foreign aid, technology transfer, or the like.

The way dignitaries handle gift-giving may not be directly applicable to most work settings; nevertheless, the transaction can and should be applied to our work relationships. How? Making your gift a valuable contribution to your partners can advance the work of any relationship.

Your contribution can be anything that has value to the other parties or to your joint endeavor: evidence of your talents, special information to which you have access, an immediate use of your network of contacts to get something done, etc. When you contribute up front, you demonstrate that generosity is your normal way of operating. If you also make it known that you don't expect an immediate payoff, but do expect such contributions to produce extraordinary payoffs later, you effectively "prime the pump" of the relationship and encourage others to open with contributions as well. There's no better way to establish a norm of contributing in a new team than to take the first step yourself.

Think about it. When individuals expect to see a payoff before they offer their contribution, we see their efforts—no matter how laudatory—as a simple "transaction." People with TeamWisdom know that in collaborations, the most worthwhile payoffs usually lag well behind the contributions. To establish a norm of giving within a team, people with TeamWisdom know it's not just polite to open with a contribution, it's smart.

Personal Challenge

Reflect on the last time that you entered a new collaboration. How did your "normal" behavior contribute to establishing a relationship norm? What was that norm? Was it to contribute or to wait and see (i.e., to withhold)? Did you attempt to specify the payoff before anything else? How can you conceive your next relationship as an avenue for mutual contribution instead of simple "transaction?"

Team Challenge

Assess the team's current status and ask the teammates individually what immediate contribution they can make that will help advance the team's or a teammate's efforts? Record, share and discuss your responses, then make your contributions as soon as possible.

TeamWisdom Applied

Two Decades of Contributing in New Relationships

Twenty years ago I heard a story of a successful young lawyer in my town. Every morning, according to the story, he would read a number of different newspapers with a pair of scissors, index cards, paper clips, and pen at hand. He would clip articles that reminded him of someone he knew, attach a note saying "Thought of you when I read this," and carry the whole bunch to work where his assistant would stuff and address envelopes and mail them. Every day he did this. Recently I worked with this lawyer in a meeting about developing leaders in central Texas. He is now a prominent leader in the business community having served as an aide to a Texas governor and Chairman of the Chamber of Commerce among many other positions. In my mail the very next day after the meeting came a large brown envelope containing a book on the topic of community leadership and transformation. Paper-clipped to the book-jacket was his card and scrawled across the card in his handwriting was "Christopher, Enjoyed our meeting."

The Gift of a "Present Hero"

"Present Heroes" seize opportunities to maximally serve their teams and themselves simultaneously.

Imagine yourself driving through a quiet countryside towards town. Rounding a curve in the narrow country road, you come upon a traffic jam. Cars in front of you are backed up around the next curve. The cars coming towards you are evenly spaced out and accelerating up to speed, as if they have just stopped for something.

As you approach the center of the jam, you notice cars in both lanes pulling off to get around something in the road. When you reach the center of congestion, you spy a large mattress lying across the road. Apparently, it's fallen out of a truck. What do you do?

This story comes from a professor in Great Britain. And he did as everyone else did: He pulled halfway off the little two-lane road, drove around the mattress, and then drove back into his lane. Once back on the road—a frustrating five minutes behind schedule—he accelerated and headed for his office.

As a result of this incident, however, the professor found himself pondering several questions as he approached his office:

Question: How many people were put how far behind schedule?
Answer: Hundreds of people, thousands of minutes.

Question: How much collective expense might have been saved if one person had cared enough about the group of motorists to stop and move the mattress off the road?
Answer: All of the expense.

Question: What was missing?
Answer: One "hero" willing to save everyone a lot while personally expending very little.

This true story, documented and studied by the professor, has been labeled The Theory of the Missing Hero. The hero is "missing" because no one came to the rescue of the group. The travelers "saved" themselves instead of making a much larger save, a gift to the whole group.

Consider two mindsets. The drivers could just as easily have seen their self-interest best served by (1) avoiding the mess or by (2) investing in fixing it for everybody. "Present Heroes" are persons who remain mindful of the abundance they enjoy as members of their communities/teams/families and assume it's usually in their own self interest to invest a little personal energy to help the group. When it comes to meeting individual and group needs, our willingness to think in terms of "both/

and" instead of "either/or" is a strong indicator of our personal TeamWisdom.

Personal Challenge

Choose one of the dozens of annoyances you have been wishing "someone" would take care of—a safety hazard, a coworker's difficult behavior, a team agreement that has been sliding, an inefficient work process that needs redesigning—and just take care of it yourself.

Hint: Effective Present Heroes simply demonstrate responsible choices and think in terms of service. Their actions are neither self-righteous nor attention seeking.

Team Challenge

Present Heroes seize opportunities to maximally serve their teams and themselves simultaneously. Discuss with each other the last time a team member acted as a Present Hero. How can you acknowledge this person? What obstacles or challenges does the team face right now that could use the intervention of a Present Hero or two?

TeamWisdom Quoted

"These teams are passionate about their work. In fact, the people on these kinds of teams don't view their work as 'work.' They view it as fun. They are addicted to it. They don't think about anything else. They want to talk about it, think about it, and do it all day long—and they want to be around people who feel the same way."

Harold J. Leavitt, professor at the
Stanford Graduate School of Business[3]

Master Your Intentions

For extraordinary TeamWisdom, discipline yourself
to examine both conscious and unconscious intentions.

In U.S. culture, when we claim to "intend" to do something, we are usually making a conscious pledge, or stating a goal. However, "intention" is always both conscious and unconscious. And the majority of our behaviors are actually controlled unconsciously. If you doubt this, just recall the last time you consciously sent blood to your gastrointestinal system to grab some sugar or protein and report to your muscles with it.

Unconscious drives, goals, desires, visions, dreams, urges, fears, images, thoughts, sounds, feelings, sensations, and intuitions operate in all of us all of the time. They form the basis of our unconscious intentions. And, they are extremely powerful. To illustrate, when was the last time you consciously pledged to get along with a sibling, to keep a New Year's resolution, to resolve a conflict with an associate, and then, completely blown it? The failure may not have resulted because your intention was weak or unclear. It may have been that your counter-intentions—conscious or unconscious—overpowered the conscious part of the equation.

When you announce an intention and an associate reminds you, "The road to hell is paved with good intentions," she could be signaling that she perceives more about your unconscious intentions than you do. I've noticed that many people with extraordinary TeamWisdom work hard at maintaining awareness of both their unconscious and their conscious intentions. They do this by reflecting (often through meditating or writing) on the differences between their conscious intentions and their actions, results, and perceptions. Any incongruence between one's conscious intentions and one's actual behavior holds information about unconscious intentions. People with TeamWisdom use this awareness to fuel self-discovery and develop cooperation skills and harness these forces to build powerful integrity.

A practice tip: Next time you catch yourself taking words back by saying "I didn't mean it," reflect on how you really might have meant it at some level. For my money, time spent examining our intentions is a far better investment than time spent in routine goal setting or planning that addresses only conscious objectives.

Personal Challenge

Examine and clarify your intentions for several upcoming meetings, relationship encounters, or even solo activities. Get specific and focused on your intentions. What results do you intend to achieve with each activity? Attention to specificity and clarity helps us communicate with the unconscious mind. After each activity, check in with yourself to see how closely your intentions were met. If they were not, ask yourself what counter-intentions you might also have been holding. Did you allow someone else's intentions (conscious or not) to become more powerful than yours?

Team Challenge

For extraordinary TeamWisdom to emerge in a group, team members must discipline themselves to examine both conscious and unconscious intentions. Have teammates ask themselves, "What are my intentions for participating in this team's activities? Will my intentions, both conscious and unconscious, lead the team closer to its goals?" Record your responses in a shared space and discuss them. If you see that anyone's intentions are not in alignment with the group's goal, use your TeamWisdom to choose how best to change relationships on the team.

TeamWisdom Applied

An Amazingly Intentional Team

Having the department training budget reduced opened an extraordinary window of opportunity for a group of IBM PC assemblers in a new manufacturing facility in Research Triangle Park, North Carolina. The department manager suggested that the team itself take over orienting newly hired assemblers and training them to work on the manufacturing line.

With the goal of "saving our jobs by increasing our plant's competitiveness," the team took on the challenge. One member had studied to be a teacher, so he researched adult learning processes and designed a curriculum that fellow assemblers could deliver. Another loved research and she searched plant records to capture the essential quality statistics and information new hires needed to know. A third member aspired to management and used the opportunity to map and catalog the plant processes and procedures so they could be rapidly assimilated by anyone, new hire or not. A fourth member applied her interior design interests and turned a corner of the plant into a beautiful learning facility complete with whiteboard walls, carpeted floor, modular furniture, and an audio-visual system.

The team's new-hire orientation message opened with the presenter standing over a cardboard box containing a new PC, saying: "How good is 'good enough'? Is 99.99 percent out-of-box quality good enough? How would you like to be the one proud family out of 10,000 that brings home their new IBM PC, plugs it in, and nothing happens? Does that qualify as 'good enough'?"

Living and Working "on" Purpose

If you want to take 100-percent responsibility for a successful life, discover or choose your life's purpose and go for it.

TeamWisdom is much more than a set of techniques. It's a way of being that extends way past the job of getting smart people to work together. People with TeamWisdom have developed a heightened appreciation for productive relationships as a means for advancing their own purpose in life and at work.

Many wise teachers throughout history have celebrated the virtues of discovering a reason for being—a life purpose. Career counselors say that discovering purpose helps people find their best work and greatest success. Business experts say that to thrive a business must have a purpose beyond just making money.

What does finding a purpose have to do with TeamWisdom?

Well, the clarity of direction that comes from being "on" purpose—be it inventing new technology, developing leaders, serving the sick and hurt, or leading people through the difficulties of change—is highly empowering. We experience people, things, and information with new and clear perspective once we are "on" purpose.

When we live and work with the conscious intention that accompanies purpose, we magnetize ourselves to attract three types of people:

▶ People who can help us learn what we need to learn

▶ People who can help us achieve our purpose (since our purposes are almost always larger than we can achieve by ourselves in one lifetime)

▶ People who will be served by our purpose

People who live "on" purpose have developed their skills at collaboration to gain these benefits. They are folks whose jobs here on earth are bigger—often much, much bigger—than they are. If you don't have this sense of purpose in your life or work, I invite you to take a moment to imagine how it would feel to know with certainty that there is a clear need for you and your unique abilities in this world. It's true.

Personal Challenge

To discover or choose your purpose in life and work, reflect on these questions. Then begin to design your life and work to support your answers:

- ► If you were to inherit $1,000,000/month, tax free, for the rest of your life, but you could only receive the money if you still worked 40 hours a week, providing something of great value to the world, what would you do?

- ► When you look around at the world you live in, what do you see that needs doing—that no one else sees— that you are singularly qualified to do?

- ► What application of your intelligence, passion, and abilities excites you?

Team Challenge

To take 100-percent responsibility for a successful life, discover or choose your life's purpose and go for it. Take 20 minutes to prepare a statement of your life's purpose and share it with people in your team. Then give them an opportunity to help you achieve it. How can the pursuit of your life's purpose mutually benefit your teammates, the team and its goals?

TeamWisdom Quoted

"The significant business of your life is alive and well, awaiting discovery, within your very soul. You and I were born to come into ourselves as complete and distinctive persons. Accepting this, we build a valuable life. This is the hidden, undergirding occupation beneath anyone's meaningful purpose."

Marsha Sinetar, in To Build the Life You
Want, Create the Work You Love[4]

2

Creating Powerful Partnerships

TEAMWISDOM INVITATION

People who can consistently create powerful relationships at work are people who are good teamworkers. In my experience, their central characteristics include:

▶ Trustworthiness (keeping promises and commitments)

▶ Commitment to common goals and targets (refusing to slip from them because of external attractions)

▶ The ability to listen and be open to others' ideas

▶ The ability to present a personal viewpoint logically and objectively

▶ The ability to self-criticize and receive others' feedback with equanimity

▶ The ability to motivate others (free of manipulation)

▶ The ability to complete tasks and achieve results

In other words, people who create powerful relationships at work are people with good leadership skills.

Developing powerful collaborations at work requires us to focus on personal relationships—that is, the human side of conducting business. Experience has taught me that I achieve my greatest success when I provide others with opportunities to excel by using their special skills and talents.

In today's economy, organizations can remain adaptive and agile only by maintaining powerful and successful relationships with other organizations. Part of this process includes acknowledging that people see things differently and contribute to partnerships differently. Homogeneity and unity leads very soon to complacency and decline, particularly in a global marketplace. Different perspectives are integral to organizational health and to partnering success.

Ten years ago, I saw differences and disagreement in my teams as a negative sign. Today, I find myself quite worried when everyone agrees quickly. It's usually either a sign that no one really understands the subject under discussion or that everyone is saying "yes" in order to terminate the dialogue with no intention to work on what was agreed upon.

Disagreement—and even positive conflict between partners—provides energy and depth to work and discussion. Young or inexperienced leaders tend to avoid conflict because they see it as a potential personal criticism of another, usually because they see themselves as right, often stubbornly so. They may well be right, but even when the absolute truth of a situation can be determined, the absolute truth is often not the best solution for an organizational dispute. Organizations are collections of individuals whose ways of thinking differ. Solutions that emerge out of differences are more likely to represent more of those ways of thinking and more effectively address the goals of the organization as well.

Exploring and applying the tools and principles in this chapter will help you and your teams learn to build powerful partnerships among players that bring to the table

different strengths and points of view. You will learn to
see these differences as a positive sign—a sign of dynamic
potential—of your organization's health.

OLLI-PEKKA JUHANTILA
Manager, Outsourcing
Nokia Mobile Phones
Salo, Finland

What's in It for Them?

To make yourself a powerful motivator, help
other people tell you what's in it for them to work
on a project with you.

Many leaders still carry what I would call a backward understanding of the motivation process. For who knows how long,
when a leader wanted a follower to perform a task, both the
leader and the follower expected the leader to tell the follower
what was in it for the follower to comply. No one questioned
the logic of this transaction. That was just the way it was done.

If we examine this kind of "enrollment" transaction from
outside the convention, however, it's a pretty funny way to get
people to do things. The truth is, when one person is looking
for another's commitment to high performance, it's much
smarter (and a lot easier) for the first person to tap into the
second person's existing motivation, instead of dictating that
motivation. Even if the follower's motivation is hidden, it's
there. And it's the follower's motivation that fuels her performance, not the leader's.

Examine the logic contained in the following five statements:

1. Everyone alive has hopes, dreams, and wants for themselves.

2. People who have no hopes, dreams, or wants are dead.

3. When people get out of bed and go to work, they have linked what they are going to do that day to their hopes, dreams, and wants in a way that makes sense to them. Or they wouldn't get up, would they?

4. Therefore, all of us have our own excellent reasons for investing in work projects—even if we have learned to deny or hide those reasons, sometimes even from ourselves.

5. The best way for me to serve fellow workers is to help them uncover and focus on their own motivations— even if they attempt to convince me they have none.

If you agree with this logic, you can stop trying to dictate other people's motivation today. The next time you need to motivate someone try asking, "What's in it for you to work on this project with this team?" and *keep the other person in conversation* until he comes up with the personal benefits that motivate him.

This method is simple, powerful, and responsible. Watch how it works.

Personal Challenge

Practice uncovering existing motivation in yourself before you try to help others uncover it in themselves. Think of a task you have to do that usually requires extra motivation, like taking out the garbage, folding laundry, mowing the lawn, or emptying the dishwasher. Ask yourself, "What's in it for me to do this?" Note your response. If this response does not move you to action, probe further by asking yourself, "What else does it do for me?" Pursue these questions until you find yourself moving to action. Note what actually got you going. Your motivation might have been buried under several unappealing layers. Your true motivation is always to get something you want (even if you believe you have to do something you don't want to do to get it).

Team Challenge

Ask others, "What's in it for you to work with us on this task?" Remember, if the first answer doesn't appear to be moving to the person, feed that answer back and follow-up with, "What else does it do for you?" Repeat this feedback loop until you both hear how this person's potential contribution to the group is connected to the future she envisions.

TeamWisdom Quoted

"What was clear with everyone we sat down with was that they were passionate about what they were doing. They loved to talk about it. Also, the job today is so enormously demanding that you have to have a high energy level . . . . When the passion gives way, that's when you know it's time for that person to move on."

Thomas Nef, author of *Lessons from the Top*[1]

It's in Your Interest to Be Helpful to Other People

The more helpful you are to other people, the more they will give you access to what motivates them.

Have you heard the story about the researcher who joined the organization disguised as a laborer in order to study organizational relationships as an insider? After months of work, this researcher had not collected much data because the others were not opening up to him very much. Then, in an after-work hockey game, he happened to score the goal that won the tournament for the company team. After this event, people became much more open to him, sharing tons of information they had not shared before. It was as if his helping the team win had flipped the switch on information flow.

People with TeamWisdom flip such switches all the time with their ability to help and serve others. It's not that they subordinate themselves to others. Neither do they give up their own pursuits and help others exclusively. But they do learn as much as they can about other people's goals, and they do look for opportunities to help others move closer to achieving them. In other words, people with TeamWisdom demonstrate allegiance to others. And it's this allegiance that earns them deeper access to previously unshared information and ideas.

The great philosopher/inventor, Buckminster Fuller, taught that the best way for one person to win is not by making others lose, but by making others win too. He taught from the 1940's until his death that the more people a person helps to win, the more people that person can expect will help her win. Fuller's teaching was in the forefront of a growing body of literature about the power and humanity of "servant leadership."[2] Being a servant leader means helping one's followers become successful, instead of expecting followers to serve one's personal success.

Personal Challenge

Do your partners and teammates provide you with access to their thoughts because they experience you as a person who helps them achieve their goals? Listen carefully to your associates to learn what is truly important to them. Check in with yourself to determine your level of commitment to them. If this level of commitment is low, ask yourself why. If it is high, ask yourself how you are willing to help. Then offer that help.

Team Challenge

When team members look out for each other's interests, the entire team benefits. Spend an hour sharing your personal goals with each other and learning about the goals of your teammates. Ask yourselves, "How can we help each other win?"

TeamWisdom Applied

One Leader Who Watches Out for the Interests of Teammates

John was a software development manager who had been approved for a larger assignment by his director and vice president. He only had to pass the CEO's interview. First the CEO asked John what was in it for him to take the assignment. Then he thought through the challenges with John. The CEO wanted to know if John had carefully assessed his own abilities and capacity to take on more work. Then he asked John if he had the support of the people who reported to him and his peers, and if they would continue to get the attention they needed from him. Next, the CEO asked John if his family obligations could be met given the hours and travel required by this new assignment. Finally, the CEO shared his own motivation: "John, I want you to succeed in this role for two critical reasons. First, yes, I want the company to succeed. But just as importantly, I want you to succeed because if you don't, and it was because you weren't ready or we didn't think through the assignment, then your career could be hurt and we could lose you. I don't want that to happen."

Protect the Interests of Other People

Discover the interests of your teammates and disallow
any action that might disparage those interests.

Remember the last time the integrity police cornered you about something? Maybe you got caught telling a lie or violating a commitment. Wasn't it awful? But then didn't you feel better when you did the right thing? Whenever you or anyone else in a team chooses to play the role of integrity cop, it can make others uncomfortable. But it also makes a major contribution to the strength of the team.

In our research on partnering between groups and organizations, we have often observed at least one member in a well-functioning group whose theme song goes something like this: "I never know which direction I'm going to be pointing my finger when I come to work. Some days, I'm addressing my own company saying, 'We can't do that to our partners!' Some days, I'm addressing our partners saying, 'Don't treat us that way!' "

The folks who occupy the position of integrity police are important to the maintenance of relationships between partners. Our research indicates that they possess three primary characteristics:

1. They display an endless capacity to record and remember both the explicit agreements and implicit expectations made between partners.

2. They exhibit extraordinary mindfulness of how entering a partnership exposes vulnerabilities on both sides. They don't hesitate to sound the alarm when one partner's actions threaten to violate another's interests or boundaries.

3. They have irrepressible urges to "call it" when any party initiates action that could violate any other party.

Such people have extraordinary TeamWisdom! From them, we can all learn the importance of discovering "what's in it" for each of our teammates. We learn that discovery and mindfulness of the whole scope of primary interests helps all members of the team protect their outcomes from the self-absorbed and potentially unintegrated actions of others.

Personal Challenge

Think about the way you usually behave in collaborative relationships. Do you play the role of integrity police? Or do you close your eyes when other people's interests and boundaries are violated. Consider at least one collaborative relationship where you know another person's interests are being violated. Decide how you can best contribute to the integrity of the relationship. And do it.

Team Challenge

Gather together, think about each teammate's individual interests in the team's efforts, and then list those interests. List all explicit agreements intended to protect the interests of teammates. Also attempt to discover and list implicit expectations. Implicit expectations are unspoken standards about how people "should" behave in relationships. For instance: "They *should* treat me with respect," most people would say. Now, ask the following questions about the lists you have produced:

- ▶ Are anyone's interests being violated (intentionally or not)?

- ▶ If so, what's the most productive way to "call" the offender(s)?

- ▶ How do team members need to be made more aware of each other's interests, vulnerabilities, relationship expectations, and agreements?

TeamWisdom Quoted

"Much of who and what I am, along with whatever level of personal success I've achieved, was shaped by my athletic experiences in high school and college. In particular, it was my high-school basketball coach who taught me two lessons that I still practice today. First, he had me write down specific personal goals before each season started. And he insisted that I look at them every single day. Second, he convinced me that a critical part of my success was helping to make my teammates better—that I could win just as much recognition and have just as much fun passing the ball as scoring myself. Since I was the team's leading scorer, this reasoning was hard to swallow. But again, I followed his advice and good things happened: We won more games, my teammates liked me better, and I had more fun."

Robert Knowling, Vice President,
Network Operations, U.S. West[3]

The Miracle of Efficient Gifts

Give favors that cost little, yet provide real value.
Ask for favors with the same principle in mind.

Is it easy for you to grant a small favor to someone you have just met? Are you just as willing to ask a favor of someone you have just met?

Most people find it much easier to grant a favor than to ask for one. However, people with TeamWisdom know that asking for a favor actually grants the other person a favor. Asking for a favor communicates to the other person that they are impor-

tant to us, that we depend on them, and that we are even willing to owe them one. People with TeamWisdom understand
that the person who asks for the first favor sets the tone for the
collaboration.

Most people enjoy being asked for small favors because it
enables them to serve. A principle of collaborative communication is at work here: When one asks for or offers help, she ac-
knowledges her interdependence. You can actually launch into
teamwork by making either a simple request or a simple offer.
How then do we get the most out of asking for and granting
favors? Economist Kenneth Boulding recommends that leaders
focus on "efficient gifts." Boulding defines efficient gifts as
favors that cost the giver little or nothing to provide, yet provide great value to the receiver. Examples include:

- ▶ Early warning of an impending threat or opportunity
- ▶ Introductions and referrals
- ▶ Welcome feedback that reinforces or corrects a
  course of action
- ▶ Temporarily covering another's post
- ▶ Receiving and forwarding messages
- ▶ Holding doors open
- ▶ Proofreading a document
- ▶ Answering a simple (or maybe even silly-sounding)
  question thoughtfully

There are an infinite number of ways we can offer assis-
tance for little or no cost to ourselves. It was Boulding's belief
that efficient gifts add more value—even in the business
world—than transactional exchanges. It's also been said that
miracles are interpersonal in nature. In that light, people with
TeamWisdom are both smart business people and miracle
workers.

Personal Challenge

Reflect on how deserving you feel you are to ask for and receive what you want. Get clear about it! Then ask a favor of someone you just met or of someone you don't know very well who you would like to know better. Ask without any preamble about how you will do them a favor later. (That would turn their giving of the favor into an exchange.) Just ask straight out and be willing to receive.

Team Challenge

Begin a discussion designed to answer this question: "How often do you ask for or offer help to each other?" Try to create an environment where favors are asked for and offered more frequently, and then chart your movement towards increased interdependence.

TeamWisdom Applied

An Efficient Gift That Keeps on Giving

Meri Walker and Christopher Avery became associated through Meri's efficient gift to Christopher that continues to produce rewards to this day. A few years ago, Dan Gately, a purchasing manager at DTM Corporation sought team-building help for a critical project team. He contacted Meri and her company, Between the Lines Strategic Communications. Meri couldn't take on the work herself, but she put DTM in touch with Christopher and Partnerwerks. Partnerwerks gained a new client, the DTM project team exceeded everyone's expectations, and Meri received a nice thank-you gift from Christopher. More importantly than any of this, perhaps, is that Meri and Christopher became collaborators.

Celebrate the Successes of Other People

When you routinely celebrate the successes of other people,
you program yourself to expect success—from yourself and
from other people.

"Don't envy the successes of others!" An important partnering principle is embedded in this advice that we have heard since childhood. But what does envying other people's successes have to do with partnering? Plenty. Envy displays and reinforces the assumption that there is a limited amount of success in the world. To envy the success of others suggests we believe that the other person's success means there is less success available for us.

When I hear people speak with jealousy, envy, or outright antagonism about another person's good fortune, I'm saddened. Such comments also suggest that when others receive an opportunity or success before we do, it's evidence that the world is unfair and unjust. While this assumption has little objective validity, it is pervasive (and promoted by many sectors of our society). Believing the world is unjust filters our perception, and pretty soon, we see unjust actions everywhere.

Consider the following story of utter resentment. My friend, Steve, scored a hole-in-one recently while golfing with some buddies. A week later, one of those buddies bumped into Steve's older (and highly competitive) brother, who remarked with sincerity how "sorry" he was to run into Steve's buddy because he hadn't believed Steve's story and was "afraid" the buddy might verify it. This type of behavior is rampant in present day organizations. We have witnessed senior executives attempting to motivate employees by declaring hatred for a successful competitor. Peer managers use the politics of resentment at all levels of organizations.

People with TeamWisdom behave quite differently. They fertilize the ground in order to grow unlimited successes by always celebrating the wins and successes of others. And, in so doing, they perceive—and create—a world of unlimited abundance for themselves and others.

Personal Challenge

Try this response to success for fun at first, then see if it really works for you. When success comes to those around you, celebrate their good fortune and chant this mantra silently to yourself, "Success surrounds me all the time." Then watch how it does surround you.

Team Challenge

Recognize one or more successes your team has achieved this week. Celebrate them as a group. The celebration can be simple or extravagant, but make it fun! Put yourselves on the lookout for more and more success as you celebrate.

> ### TeamWisdom Quoted
>
> *"Share success: No individual or business can lead or succeed alone. Sharing success sustains success."*
>
> Jeannette Galvanek, President and CEO, Talent Alliance[4]

Appreciate Conflict

Viewing conflicts thoroughly is the TeamWisdom challenge. Operating with clarity is the reward.

One summer vacation I spent a week with leadership writer and TeamWisdom master, Professor Warren Bennis. The occasion was a learning session about group genius. At one point, conflict arose among the 50 or more participants concerning the direction of the session. During the discussion that ensued I was treated to several lessons in TeamWisdom:

- ▶ There is tremendous power in conducting ourselves so that the people in our presence (teammates, partners, or employees) feel free to express satisfaction or dissatisfaction with how we (and they) are investing time and attention—even when we are an expert in what the group is doing.

- ▶ When disagreements arise in a relationship, it pays to treat them as an opportunity to learn. It's unwise to squelch disagreement, cover it up, or take offense— even when we are an expert in what the group is doing.

- ▶ New opportunities will become available when we are willing to let go of our own agendas and create new ones—even when we are an expert in what the group is doing.

- ▶ Like a good punter in football, or like Michael Jordan leaving the foul line for a spectacular dunk, it's smart to create "hang time" for a workgroup. It can be wise for a leader to label a disagreement as "important" and then allow someone else to offer a new perspective that helps to resolve the disagreement—even when we are an expert in what the group is doing.

- ▶ Nothing substitutes for listening. Listen for the "truth in the room" by observing both your reactions and those of the group to each new speaker especially when we are an expert in what the group is doing.

Remember that any upset, fear, or conflict, when *thoroughly* viewed, will disappear. Whether we practice this in ourselves or within our groups, this truth is the key to appreciating conflict. This principle cannot be repeated enough: *any* upset, fear, or conflict, when thoroughly viewed, *will* disappear. People with TeamWisdom have a talent for confronting and viewing every upset exactly "as it is."

Personal Challenge

Thoroughly view at least one fear, upset, or conflict that has been plaguing you in one of your relationships. Examine it until it disappears and is replaced by powerful clarity. If it's a personal upset or fear, challenge yourself to wade through the quagmire. Upsets can only be clarified when fully experienced, not avoided.

Team Challenge

Identify a conflict, fear, or upset in your team. Invite team members to articulate as many different perspectives about the upset as possible. A perspective is neither an attempt to argue nor an attempt to resolve a position. It's a way of describing the conflict "as it is." Listen together for the "truth in the room." Don't plan a course of action until you have seen, heard, or felt this truth together.

TeamWisdom Quoted

"My management team recently agreed to set aside unstructured time to ask itself how it is leading, to raise questions about what isn't working personally or at a process level, and to identify what we should be working on. We can't afford to let conflict slide until it gets so big it's harder to handle, so we're trying to make conflict discussions and resolutions as natural as eating."

Don Kovalevich, President and CEO,
Houston Cellular Telephone Company

Distinguish Criticism from Feedback

"Constructive" criticism is still criticism. Instead of
criticizing, "feed back" your responses with compassion.

Our addiction to criticizing others is a huge block to effectively giving feedback. When we criticize, even if we choose our words with care, we are likely to assign others to a specific, potentially harmful, status. We are likely to assign others, for instance, to the status of being "wrong." No one likes to be labeled "wrong." Most people get defensive when they are labeled, even when sure they are not "wrong." And what's more important, defensive people block messages. Unless you are trying not to be understood, then, criticism is not an effective communication strategy. And it doesn't help to call it "constructive" either. Saying something like, "I'm telling you this for your own development, your design is all wrong" isn't going to produce positive results. Criticism is criticism. It blocks understanding.

So, what replaces "constructive criticism" for the responsible team member? Something I call "compassionate revelation" (i.e., telling your truth with compassion) works quite well. In fact, compassionate revelation is the essence of effective feedback. You practice it by pointing out the consequences of another person's actions. The trick is to feed the consequences of someone's actions back to them truthfully and compassionately.

Say you have a person reporting to you named Mary, and Mary places a proposal on your desk that, in your opinion, will have to be rewritten. Consider the following two responses to her work. You decide which one will get a better response and why:

▶ "Mary, I'm sorry to have to tell you this even though it's for your own good. Your proposal is lousy. It will have to be completely rewritten if you want a chance of getting the business."

▶ "Mary, in my experience, this proposal is not going to produce the result that I think you want. Let's talk about it and determine what it might take to get the business."

Personal Challenge

Notice when you begin to assign someone the status of being "wrong." Stop yourself and remain silent until you can compassionately feed back to the person the effects of her behavior on you or your teammates.

Hint: Criticism usually includes phrases like "You are (favorite judgment here)" or "This is (favorite judgment here)." Feedback includes phrases such as "When you (specific action here), I (your compassionately revealed response here)."

Team Challenge

Discuss with your team the distinction between criticism and feedback. Remember that most people have been told that constructive criticism is a good thing. Explain compassionate revelation and begin using it with teammates instead of criticism.

TeamWisdom Applied

Someone Who Received Honest Feedback and Grew

Susan worked with a group of individuals who engaged in lots of squabbles. They would regularly come to Susan individually and share their conflicts with her. Wanting to help, Susan dutifully listened to each of the parties individually and made suggestions about how to settle the conflicts. Unfortunately, the squabbles didn't abate. The conflicts grew worse, the individuals' abilities to resolve them seemed to decrease, and the individuals came to Susan more frequently with even petty complaints. Susan eventually grew weary and sought advice. She discovered that instead of helping, she was actually fanning the flames by getting involved in the interpersonal disputes of her teammates. She decided to take a new stance. When one of the people who reported to her came with a complaint about another team member, Susan responded with the following: "Sounds like you have a problem. There are two ways I'm willing to be involved. First, the two of you can come to me together and I'll mediate your conflict. Second, if you want to increase your own responsibility for the quality of your relationships, I'll coach you to learn how to have more productive relationships." Over the next six months, the conflicts ceased and morale in the group rose significantly.

What about Their Integrity?

*Practice tit-for-tat to make collaborators aware of
their responsibility for the relationship.*

It's in your best interest to carry on collaborative relationships with the utmost integrity. Never be the first to defect.

If you are like so many people I talk to, the above statement makes perfect sense to you. It may, however, leave you feeling vulnerable to others' defections. It may cause you to ask questions like, "What about them?!" and "Am I supposed to stand by and let others defect on me first?"

Although trying to second-guess others or trying to control them is wasted effort, it doesn't mean we are helpless in our relationships. As we concern ourselves less with predicting the behavior of others and more with making our own behavior correspond with what we say, the people we deal with will follow our lead. The way we relate to others, then, can effect their actions. That's right, *their* actions. Here's how.

Learn and apply the "tit-for-tat" strategy referred to in the previous chapter. There are two rules to tit-for-tat: (1) Always cooperate on your first interaction with someone, and (2) on each successive interaction, follow the other person's lead.

Based on Robert Axelrod's research of game theory[5], tit-for-tat is a workable, proven formula for increasing cooperation under competitive conditions. Derived from game theory, computer science, and evolutionary psychology, tit-for-tat is the simplest and most straightforward strategy for (1) maximizing the potential of the relationship for each party and (2) getting out of a relationship quickly if the actions of others put you at risk of losing.

Think about it. If the other party follows the same strategy, both of you will make trusting opening moves when the relationship begins. Then each successive interaction will be one of trust, mutual support, and collaboration, and neither party will defect on the other. If, on the other hand, the other party does not cooperate with you (i.e., if the person breaks an agreement or takes advantage of you in some other way), then your next move, following tit-for-tat, will be to refuse to cooperate with them.

Tit-for-tat can be an effective way of building a relationship in the following ways:

> ► In a new relationship, always be willing to make a
> contribution to the team that, if not matched by others,
> will not leave you feeling at risk. Then do what you
> said you would do, and see if others make similar
> contributions to the team. If they do, then tit-for-tat
> rules suggest that you keep making contributions to

the team. If others don't contribute, then tit-for-tat rules suggest you should reconsider your original contribution.

▶ When you choose to remain "locked into" a relationship (like staying with a job that requires you to work with others), make sure the other parties understand that (1) you will never defect on them, and (2) they can be in charge of the quality of the relationship: If they support you, you will support them; if they defect on you, you will withdraw support for them. Then follow through.

▶ Don't tolerate defections. But don't be overly punitive or self-righteous, either. Getting even is not a move in tit-for-tat. When you match the other party's defection, always do so with equal or *lesser* force. If you match the other party's defection with greater force, the other party is likely to take your move as a signal to escalate.

Personal Challenge

Choose a relationship in which (1) defections sometimes occur and often turn into escalations, and (2) you are committed to increasing collaboration. Commit to adopting tit-for-tat as your own strategy. As you think things through, consider carefully what you need to change about your behavior to make the strategy viable.

Team Challenge

After you have thought through how to change your behavior, solicit a conversation with a partner (a team member, colleague, or family member) about your dissatisfaction with how you have responded in the past and demonstrate your intent to respond differently in the future.

TeamWisdom Quoted

"Whole Foods is a social system. It's not a hierarchy. We don't have lots of rules handed down from head- quarters in Austin. We have lots of self-examination going on. Peer pressure substitutes for bureaucracy. Peer pressure enlists loyalty in ways that bureaucracy doesn't."

John Mackey, cofounder and CEO of Whole Foods[6]

End with the Beginning in Mind

When ending a partnership, call to mind the
collaboration when it was at its most prosperous.

I don't know why people so seldom end relationships well.

Maybe it's because we all want so much to win—and end- ings are associated with losing. Maybe it's because we are em- barrassed that we don't know how to derive any more benefits from a partnership. Maybe we are embarrassed because of unkept promises, real or imagined. Maybe we are upset because someone didn't live up to our expectations.

Whatever the reasons, when collaborations or partnerships come to an end, most people start jockeying for position, poli- ticking, and blaming negative circumstances on partners. Sometimes endings even explode into battles.

Were we to describe the phenomenon analytically, we might say that collaborative behavior tends to diminish as the outer edge of a contract's time horizon comes into view. No matter how lucrative the venture may have been for both parties, by the time the end actually comes, it's common for one or both parties to want to get far away from the other. Psychologists use this aphorism to describe bad ends: We don't break up because we are fighting; we fight because we are breaking up.

I won't pretend we can do much to avoid endings. They are as inevitable as beginnings. But I have observed that we can improve the quality of endings by avoiding three things:

1. Burning bridges
2. Harming reputations
3. Being inhumane to oneself and others

In my experience, we can practice TeamWisdom when it comes time to end a relationship by taking the following five steps:

1. End the collaboration by bringing to mind the positive intentions and positive results that the partnership produced.
2. Thank your partners for the opportunities, results, and trust they provided you.
3. Explain that you don't see any motivation to continue investing in the relationship and that this does not mean that either party should attempt to cause a loss for the other.
4. Negotiate fairly and compassionately during the dismantling of infrastructure and the redistribution of responsibilities. Pay your fair share or more of these expenses. If either party feels threatened, engage the services of a facilitator.
5. If the other party exhibits difficult end-game behavior, show compassionate provocability and strive for resolution by de-escalating rather than escalating.

Personal Challenge

Reflect on one or more of your collaborations that ended poorly or in conflict. Bring to mind the best days of that collaboration. Now envision a way to use your *current* TeamWisdom to craft a more responsible endgame. Keep this vision in mind the next time you begin a collaboration.

Team Challenge

Identify an approaching ending for the team. This could be either an internal or external relationship coming to a close. Discuss the five steps outlined above and how the team will follow each step to create a smooth closure.

TeamWisdom Quoted

"The actual process of creating a lot of visual effects for a movie doesn't worry me. I worry about creating an environment in which people can perform at that level and not be totally burned out when they're done. Three months from now, we'll all be working as a team on another project. You can't afford to treat people like they're disposable."

Eric Brevig, Visual Effects Supervisor, Lucas Digital[7]

All Teams Need Closure

When dismantling a successful team, make sure team members "close" that chapter of their work lives so they can focus their energy on the new work before them.

Have you ever been part of an effort that ended abruptly, was canceled, or just blew up? How about one that just petered out? Were you expected to come to work the next day and act as if nothing had happened? Weird, huh?

The way some teams end can leave participants feeling incomplete, confused, or even abused. Ending this way costs the participants psychically and diminishes their productivity.

People with TeamWisdom understand teams require closure. Most teams begin ceremoniously with announcements, formations, orientations, and launches. Too many teams, however, disregard the value of a ritual ending. Without one, members are left with the loose ends of their personal investment. A lack of formal resolution shows up in foggy cognitions like, "What was that about?" "Why was I involved in that anyway?" and "Do I really want to do that again?"

If your uncle Wilbert were suddenly to drop dead, would you bury him without some kind of service? Of course not. Why not? Well, society would label you a creep. Above and beyond the pressures of social convention, however, most of us would hold a service to "pay our last respects" and, by so doing, invite closure for ourselves and others in the matter of a deceased relative.

Beyond the moral and spiritual wounds, unacknowledged endings create craters in productivity. People can't turn their attention and energy towards new goals until they have let go of the old. As a friend of mine says, all teams need either to celebrate together or to cry in their beer together. *What* they do together may not be nearly as important as the fact that they *do something* together to mark the end of their mutual investments.

To choose an appropriate vehicle for closure, ask yourself (and maybe a few others) what activity would allow members to feel "complete." The size, cost, and formality of the activity depends on the desires of the group. One of my favorite closure activities is a simple meal or meeting where each group member gets to say what he thinks about the project. Go around the table until everyone has said what's on her mind.

Personal Challenge

Search your memory for a relationship that ended without closure. When you identify one, make notes about what it would have taken for you to feel complete. Identify at least one concrete benefit you would gain from initiating closure. Would anyone else benefit from this closure?

Team Challenge

Discuss this question with your team: What closure activity should we initiate so that everyone can feel complete? Design an event that has meaning for all members of the group. Now hold the event and close the relationship so you can get on with a new project.

TeamWisdom Applied

Closure Ritual Creates a New Beginning

I recently dined at Emeril's, the New Orleans restaurant named after the famous TV chef Emeril Lagasse. We had an opening-time reservation and wedged ourselves into a packed reception area/lounge where all could view the dining room. No one was yet seated. The entire restaurant staff pored over the table-settings, checking tableware, glasses, and each others' stations for perfection. Then, at precisely 6:28, the staff huddled in the middle of the dining room—a dozen or more men and women in white jackets and black slacks, arms around each other's backs and bent over in a private meeting while all of the soon-to-be diners watched. Who knows what they said to transition from setting to serving, but after about 90 seconds, they startled us with a collective shout and exploded out of the huddle. The atmosphere became electric as the waiters lined up briefly at the reception stand, each receiving a slip of paper from the hostess and calling out a party's name, then meeting and leading the party to their table. In minutes' time, the staff, customers, dining room, and reception area transformed completely from one stage to the next. No wonder Chef Emeril is hot!

3

Collaborating "on" Purpose

TEAMWISDOM INVITATION

An organization in which everyone is collaborating powerfully and "on" purpose is a thing of beauty.

On a well-run team, team members are focused on a clearly understood, shared goal. Little or no time is spent on wheel spinning and low-yield activities. Team members get more done in less time, and technical expertise isn't the only factor fueling the team's efforts. Commitment to a common task drives the success of the team.

How do we set up and support teams to function this way? My own experience has taught me that the most powerful force for success in teamwork is intense commitment from each participant. I was at SEMATECH from 1989 to 1996, and during the early part of my tenure the company had a single, overriding, clearly articulated mission—to rescue the U.S. semiconductor industry from the threat of foreign domination. Each project we launched was designed to move the industry in the direction of that goal. To accomplish it, participants set aside their short-term parochial interests in service to the larger, overriding goal.

During my tenure with SEMATECH, I observed employees of bitter rivals (AMD and Intel, Texas Instruments and Motorola, and Digital and IBM) work together side by side. Assignees to SEMATECH had little trouble taking off their individual company hats and putting on their collective team hats. Participants were still identifiable as having come from their unique corporate cultures—Intel's culture, for instance, is famous for "constructive confrontation" and their assignees to SEMATECH certainly brought that attribute with them—but all participants were willing to work through differences because we were intensely committed to saving America's most important industry. To this day, I carry this powerful experience of synergy with me, and it fuels my vision for and participation in Nowdocs.com, the company for which I now work.

What would your organization look like if everyone was collaborating powerfully and on purpose? What does it look like now? Are people guided by a common overarching mission? Are decisions based on clear, shared values? Are people and departments making aligned contributions to larger collective wins rather than scrapping over disconnected pieces of the pie? The TeamWisdom tools and practices explored in this book are precisely what you need to answer all these questions and get your organization moving in the right direction. In the memorable words of StarTrek Captain JeanLuc Picard, "Make it so!"

MICHAEL S. OSWALD, JD
Vice President, General Counsel
and Chief Administrative Officer
NowDocs.com, Inc.

Clarity Is the Source of Power

To move forward together, establish shared clarity.

When was the last time you were in a team where the participants held different ideas about their collective task? How fast did you make progress together? If your experience is anything like mine, not very fast! Lack of shared clarity about direction gets teams stuck. When a group lacks clarity about the task at hand, it's not just easy but natural for people to lose interest in what they are doing. And once interest starts to flag, it's hard to believe the team will ever come together, much less accomplish its goals.

What does shared group clarity look like? Simple. Each member should be able to explain simply and clearly what the team is accountable for (not individual roles, but the collective purpose). The mental images behind these statements should be identical across the team. Thus when listening to each other, teammates should hear their own ideas reflected back at them. And there should be sufficient detail to assure that the ideas really are duplicated and not just approximated. When teammates communicate the same future outcomes to each other, they probably have shared clarity.

Shared clarity can be gained through early, aggressive alignment about direction. The charter, mission, deliverable, or outcome of the team's work must be clarified together through discussion and conversation. Think about the times when you accepted ambiguous direction like, "Make money!" Then think about the times when you accepted clear direction like, "By the end of the year, design a second release of our product that we can build efficiently, and, that our customers want to buy from us." In which situation were you more resourceful?

When a group, such as a project team, is temporary, it's important to align members around the collective task they are to perform. When a group, such as a department, is ongoing, it's important to align members around the ongoing purpose of the group. Either way, tasks and purposes must be clear and shared.

Personal Challenge

For one or more of your collaborative relationships, answer this question: What's the purpose of this relationship? Describe the purpose fully. Then, ask your partner or partners to answer the same question. Talk about what you each wrote until you can articulate together a common and clear description of your purpose.

Team Challenge

Ask team members to answer this question individually in writing: If we were already finished and successful, what would our outcome look like? Describe the outcome fully. Then, talk about what each person wrote until you can articulate together a common and clear description of your outcome. I guarantee this exercise will add tremendous power to your team.

TeamWisdom Applied

Team Struggle Produces Clarity

From the start, it promised to be an interesting meeting. No sooner had the Research and Development Management team begun to specify outcomes than the meeting degenerated into a blame-storm about the group's marketing counterpart. The blaming happened again as the group attempted to prioritize an agenda. Finally, participants determined that their negative feelings about marketing was the most important item they could address at the meeting. They agreed to record their thoughts on a whiteboard and spent the next hour doing so. As they moved into discussion, though, each issue they recorded met a similar dead-end.

> Frustrated to the point of distraction, the team started reviewing their analysis—and an amazing clarity began to emerge. They began to see that marketing was not their enemy—that their dilemma was an organizational issue for which their team shared responsibility. The struggle ceased, the blaming went away, and clear direction for their approach to a powerful collaboration with marketing emerged.

Come Together Over Commitment and Skills Will Follow

Select teammates for their commitment, then together find the needed skills. Select for skills, and commitment might never appear.

Conventional wisdom on teambuilding advises leaders to first attend to creating the "right" skill mix as they assemble teams. I couldn't disagree more!

Why do I disagree? Because I have observed time and time again that skills are much less critical to responsible relationships and high performance on teams than is aligned motivation, energy, enthusiasm, drive, and interest.

Don't get me wrong. I demand the best skill-fit possible for a job. But managing skill-fit is a *project management* concern, not a *team leadership* concern. It's important not to confuse the two. I have seen "teams" with all the right skills perform miserably. And I have seen teams with low skills but broad alignment and high enthusiasm perform at extraordinary levels. Haven't you? Consider an example from sports. For many years during the 1980's and 1990's the New York Yankees baseball team had the greatest talent that money could buy, but they often got beat by teams with much less talent.

Why is this the case you ask? Why didn't the New York Yankees win the World Series every year?

- ▶ Talent doesn't create teamwork, shared desire does.
- ▶ Low motivation is more infectious in teams than is high motivation. Even highly skilled freeloaders will rapidly bring a team's performance level down.
- ▶ Skilled individuals act within their roles. Committed team members do what needs to be done for the team, that is, they improvise.

What to do? If teamwork is important to you, choose team members for their motivation first, and their skills second.

Personal Challenge

Reflect on the experiences you have accumulated participating in your last few workteams. How were skills and commitment treated during the selection and start-up processes? Use your imagination to re-make one of your last negative team experiences. Imagine how things might have been different if commitment had been addressed first and skills second. Would the team have performed better? I bet it would have. Dare to give the commitment criterion *first* priority when you assemble your next team.

Team Challenge

Discuss with your team the implications of placing "commitment over skill" with regard to team performance. How do these implications work to your advantage?

TeamWisdom Applied

Commitment Wins Out Over Skill

A common theme explored by literature, film, and TV concerns how groups with lower technical abilities (and a correspondingly lower chance to succeed at a technical challenge) overcome this liability through greater passion and commitment. Review the story lines of the following movies and TV shows and realize how often commitment is represented as more powerful than skill:

- ▶ *Baa Baa Black Sheep*
- ▶ *The Dirty Dozen*
- ▶ *Hogan's Heroes*
- ▶ *The Mighty Ducks*
- ▶ *The Bad News Bears*

In each story, the principal characters are the "second rate," the outcasts, or the difficult to manage. When grouped together with an almost insurmountable challenge, the individuals form a spirited and innovative team that improvises its way to win after win. The moral to the common story line is that accomplishment and high performance is not limited to those with talent.

Teammates Don't Have to Like Each Other

You will achieve better cohesion when individual and group outcomes are aligned, rather than relying on interpersonal attractiveness.

Many teambuilders begin their work by telling themselves, "I need to get group members to like each other better, so we'll be a better team."

While interpersonal attractiveness can be valuable on teams, investing one's efforts there is actually not the most powerful strategy. Encouraging affinity to a *shared task*—instead of encouraging affinity with each other—has proven to be the fastest and surest way to create strong group cohesion.

What does this mean in practice? Instead of using techniques and exercises to promote friendships, work to get everyone to adopt a common focus so that each team member sees good reasons to work with others.

Think about it. Free market economics teaches us to act in our own self-interest. Many team experts—influenced, perhaps, by a Japanese value system—teach that individuals must subordinate their own interests for the sake of the group's success. I see a few problems with this. First, it's contradictory (and therefore unrealistic) to expect people working in competitive cultures to subordinate their self-interests to the group. And, second, there is no necessary or logical connection between subordination and successful, powerful teamwork.

A more effective practice is to use people's self interest to seed powerful teamwork. For each individual, discover how she can win when the team wins. The easiest and best way to do this is to ask. When you align individual and collective outcomes in this way, what you will have is true collaboration.

Once that is done, see if team members don't like each other better.

Personal Challenge

Think of a teammate with whom you have often felt competitive and ask yourself this question: What could we pursue as partners that would increase the likelihood of each of us reaching our desired outcomes?

Team Challenge

Begin a group discussion with the following question: What is our team's task? Make sure people are clear about the task and that everyone is committed to achieving it. In the future, when conflict or interpersonal tension arises, have everyone recall this discussion.

TeamWisdom Quoted

"Kevin O'Connor [President of DoubleClick Inc.] and I come from completely different worlds. Sometimes we don't even speak the same language. After two years we still socialize only on a limited basis, but our relationship is built on trust rather than friendship."

Wenda Harris Millard, Executive Vice President
of Marketing, DoubleClick Inc.[1]

Stop Trying to Motivate

Since motivating others is nearly impossible, stop trying. Instead, tap into the motivation that already exists in teammates.

Many of us operate under the assumption that responsible leaders motivate people. But you know what? My experience has proven this notion to be mistaken.

When we think of "motivating" someone, we think of dangling carrots out in front of the person or holding threatening sticks overhead to start the person in motion. (In fact, "motion" is "motivation," minus a few letters). The problem is, that's not leadership. It's behavioral control.

Responsible leaders tap into the *existing* motivation of those they would lead.

In responsible relationships, we move others to action without using carrots or sticks. Period. End of story. How is this done? I recommend you discern what already puts the people you are trying to lead in motion and position yourself so they can get more of what motivates them by working with you. Position yourself so they get tons of what motivates them.

How do we find out what others *already* want? Just ask them about their dreams, wants, needs, and pleasures. When you know what others want and need, you can help them achieve these things by working on your project. When you discover what people really want and need, you can serve them by keeping the focus on what they really want and need.

Sounds simple, doesn't it? It is. Just keep in mind this Team-Wisdom principle: High performance is always voluntary.

Personal Challenge

Take ten minutes to question yourself about what puts you in motion? Is there plenty of this motivating factor built into the project you are working on now? If not, what are you going to do about it?

Team Challenge

What usually gets in the way of discovering the motivation of others is our judgment of what constitutes *proper* motivation. Know what I mean? Drop your judgments about what *should* motivate your teammates and ask them, "What's in it for you to work on this team?" Listen to all the answers until you discover what really puts each person in motion. (*Hint:* Most of us have been taught to say, "Of course, I work for the money!" But leaders with TeamWisdom probe further to find out what the money does for the person. It's not usually the money but what the money can buy or do for the person that is the real motivating factor. This motivating factor beyond the money itself can be many things. A bass boat? Freedom? A new car? Prestige?)

TeamWisdom Quoted

"A fundamental ingredient of success is self-interest, which should be viewed idealistically rather than cynically. It is a powerful motivator and can be extremely effective in getting people and organizations to do good works as much as to do well. We've mobilized thousands of talented people to fight hunger not by making them feel guilty or bad about themselves, but by giving them opportunities to express themselves on behalf of a worthwhile cause. When altruism is selfish, it becomes sustainable—perhaps forever."

Bill Shore, Executive Director, Share Our Strength[2]

How Do You Know if Your Team Is "Built"?

Teams that are well constructed share direction and energy.

You can tell from a distance if a team is "built," but first you have to understand what "built" means. Stand back, scan the team as a whole, and ask yourself these two questions:

- ▶ Have teammates adopted a specific shared direction?
- ▶ Is the entire team energized?

If the answer to both these question is "yes," then you have been examining a "built" team. To achieve this status, it's best to lay the foundation early. Start by asking yourself and fellow teammates, either individually or as a group, the following important questions. Each answer amounts to one step in a five-step process designed to determine the general orientation of a team.

1. What is the team's task? What has the team been formed to do? You can't start managing direction and energy until the task has been established. Having a shared outcome (that's articulated in such a way that *no* member can win until the team wins) may be the most important distinction between a workgroup and a team. Members are energized when they know they will win when the team wins.

2. What is the benefit to each team member for committing to the team's work? Each member's answer to this question is the source of his or her energy. And remember, a team performs to the level of its *least* invested member—not to the level of its most invested.

3. Are agreements in place that allow the team to operate rapidly and efficiently? Group velocity increases in direct proportion to group members' confidence that they can interact with each other. Confidence soars when teammates see each other maintain the team's integrity or "shape." And confidence also contributes to energy.

4. Do team members share a goal that inspires them? Clear goals produce both energy and direction and are powerful tools requiring true lateral thinking.

5. Do we know what each member brings to the team? When teams inventory and honor what each member brings to the team, work can be distributed to everyone's satisfaction, and, sometimes less than obvious talents can emerge in stunning ways. For example, only after landing a bank as a client did I learn that one of my colleagues worked as a teller in college. We were able to exploit her experience in early phases of our work. Such improvisation (situational use of resources) occurs frequently in high performance teamwork.

Knowing what the team has to draw on allows team members to lean into their forward momentum.

Personal Challenge

Close your eyes and bring to mind the profile of a team in which you are currently a member. Does this team exhibit clear direction? How about collective energy? Using the five-step Team Orientation Process described above as a diagnostic tool, pinpoint any orientation problems the team might have and resolve to address them this week.

Team Challenge

As a team, work through the Team Orientation Process, conversing about each question and resolving issues as they arise. The process may take place across a couple of meetings. This kind of examination should result in group momentum towards a specific goal. If not, revisit the Team Orientation Process until this momentum is achieved.

TeamWisdom Applied

Diligent Team Orientation

A group of young, eager vice presidents were challenged by their boss (the chief executive officer) to turn themselves into a unified team. Each of the participants had a substantial history of accomplished independent management, and each saw his fellow vice presidents as rivals for resources, management attention, and rewards. To meet the CEO's challenge, however, the group agreed to sequester themselves at a retreat site for three days and talk things over.

It took the group half a day to agree on a task they might tackle as a team. Once that was accomplished, for the first time in their work together, participants began to see that it actually made sense for them to coordinate with each other. Then they moved onto a second conversation exploring individual interests. A breakthrough occurred when they discussed their individual career aspirations and found they were not—as some had supposed—in competition with each other for the same promotions! After that, participants made agreements that would support and maintain their newfound alignment and keep individuals from defecting on one another. The team returned from their retreat demonstrating a strong working relationship, a model for the rest of the company.

Who Is the Most Powerful Member of Your Team?

Teams perform to the level of their least-committed member. To predict your team's performance capacity, examine the commitment of all your partners.

Is the team leader the most powerful member of your team? Is the most inspired member the most powerful? The smartest member? Nope. None of the above. Like it or not, the most powerful member of your team is the one who cares the least about your team's task. Sorry, but that's the truth. The least-committed member of your team is the most powerful because his lack of commitment establishes a low baseline to which other team members may fall. The success—or mediocrity—of your team likely will be determined by him.

Does anyone not despise freeloaders? We have all worked with them. They are the folks who accept the rewards, but contribute minimally to the accomplishment of group tasks. Free-loading doesn't often occur on self-managed teams because the team and the freeloader would reject each other. Freeloading can only happen where team membership is mandatory.

I've heard many people say they don't let the freeloaders (least-committed people) bother them, that they ignore or work around them. Maybe it's possible to do so in highly bureau-cratic organizations, but in true team situations, such "safe" positioning costs everyone—sometimes a lot more than we want to admit.

In my experience, when a freeloader comes into a team and can't be rejected because of bureaucratic policy, the other hard-working members of the team immediately and drastically reduce their work level and channel their attention and com-mitment to other parts of their lives. Why? Because it's human nature to want to maximize our efforts. Especially as time be-comes limited, each of us wants to apply our attention to that which will produce the greatest results. Whether we say it aloud or not, everyone knows that freeloaders leverage our efforts downward, not upward.

The uncomfortable truth is this: Teams will perform to the level of their least-invested coworker. Smart team leaders and savvy team members appreciate this principle and address mo-tivation issues early, directly, and regularly. To do less may seem easier, but in the long run it could cause the demise of the team.

Personal Challenge

Think about your team, ranking the members from most to least motivated. Ask yourself who most influences the com-mitment level of the team. If this person is leveraging the pro-ductivity of the team downward, ask yourself if this is acceptable. Here's a key: If you or others grumble or complain about a freeloader, it's likely that this person's motivation level is not acceptable. See what you can do to increase this person's commitment to the team. Start by finding out how you can frame the team's work in terms of what motivates the non-committed person.

Team Challenge

No matter how high the overall commitment of the team might be, someone in every team exhibits the least commitment. Without stigmatizing any one person, acknowledge this and discuss the following questions with your team:

► Which one of us has the least to gain from our team's success and is, therefore, the least motivated?

► What can we do to raise this person's motivation?

► Now, who is the next least committed . . . ?

TeamWisdom Quoted

"Teams themselves routinely reject candidates, and it may be the case that a team doesn't become truly effective until the team members reject someone. They're saying, 'This person isn't good enough to be on our team.' They're standing up to the leader, taking ownership of their team, saying, 'Go back and try again.'"

John Mackey, CEO, Whole Foods Market[3]

Consensus

Consensus isn't about being nice. It's high-octane fuel for team direction and energy.

The word "consent" and the word "consensus" have the same root. What some people love and others hate about the process of consensus building is that it requires participants to seek each group member's sincere consent to move forward. My definition of consensus is 100-percent agreement to move forward together.

Why is consensus important to a high-performing team?

First, a high-performing team is measured by energy and direction. Without consensus, a group has no shared direction. Without consensus, people work literally at cross-purposes, canceling out each other's efforts, instead of amplifying each other's efforts.

Second, when groups pursue a direction determined by majority or authority, those who dissent (either vocally or silently) can lose energy. They lose their commitment.

Third, the effect of low commitment on teams is dramatic. As discussed in the previous section, when low commitment is present, it will always be more infectious than high commitment. The majority may "win" but the dissenters drain needed energy away from the "winners."

People with TeamWisdom know what to do when there is a difference of opinion in a team. They silence the majority and ask dissenters, "How can we change this proposal so it works for you?" Then they listen. Usually dissenters will accept the responsibility to move the group forward and will help modify the proposal so that it works for everybody. If they are not given a voice, however, this cannot happen.

The key to consensus building is steering the discussion away from "right versus wrong" arguments. Use language that doesn't vilify dissenters, such as "That works for me," or "That doesn't work for me." And, above all, keep asking the group, "What could move us forward together?"

The real value of consensus decision-making is that it creates shared direction and high energy on a team, and isn't that how we want our teams to perform?

Personal Challenge

When you hear the word "consensus," what comes to mind? Quick decision-making? Or belabored discussion? In your past team decision-making experiences, what was the level of your team's commitment when the team moved forward by consensus? Commit to build consensus on your next team by asking the dissenters, "How can we change this proposal so that it works for you?"

Team Challenge

Create a consensus continuum similar to the one below. Then, when someone makes a significant proposal effecting everyone in the team, take a quick poll of each individual. Ask teammates to rank their level of agreement from 1 to 5:

1. Unqualified yes. Move forward.
2. Perfectly acceptable. Move forward.
3. I can live with the decision of the group. Move forward.
4. I trust the group and will not block this decision, but I need to register my disagreement. Move forward.
5. I think more work is needed before deciding. Do not move forward.
6. I do not agree and feel the need to stand in the way of adopting this decision. Do not move forward.

The usual (almost always harmful) way groups make decisions is that the majority beats-up the minority until the minority withdraws. The majority then identifies this withdrawal as consent. The point of the exercise above is to include dissenters in the group. Inclusion gives dissenters a voice, which is always better than no voice at all.

TeamWisdom Quoted

"The reality at this company is that my partners and I share information all the time. So by the time we had the meeting, all I needed to say was, 'Here's the situation and here's the opportunity,' and everyone agreed."

Larry Smith, President and CEO, US Interactive[4]

Fast Consensus

Consensus is fast and easy when you have nothing to hide and don't fear losing a fight.

Some people report a strong distaste for consensus. They think it takes too much time. Group members always polarize on issues, these people say. Group members threaten to use veto power when they don't achieve their individual purposes, they add. I find these behaviors distasteful too, I have to admit. They devour time and really sap energy.

We can short-circuit this kind of behavior, however, and put into place processes that allow a team to arrive at decisions quickly. The following suggestions are designed to help teams achieve high-velocity decision-making:

1. Consider more, rather than fewer, alternatives, and generate them together. Teams that move fast know that generating lots of alternatives actually clarifies decision-making. Trying to analyze only two or three alternatives can have the effect of focusing the team on making the "right decision." All too often, the choice can appear to be between polar opposites resulting in paralysis instead of creative thought.

2. Involve more people and more points of view in the process. When a large number of participants are heard from, unique points of view emerge. This actually increases the probability of discovering creative and expansive alternatives.

3. Communicate and integrate with other parts of the organization. Teams that move fast invite other departments to participate in their planning. By coordinating in real-time with other departments, team members can avoid having to play catch-up. An added bonus is that other departments may actually suggest new and better solutions.

4. Draw on the wisdom of "gray-hairs." Teams that move fast check their thinking with mentors and coaches whose experience, intuition, and situational knowledge help the team make smart choices.

5. The secret to making quick team decisions is to establish the importance of collective action. To fast teams, getting a result and learning from it together is more important than being right. Fast teams also make sure that everyone is heard, *especially* minority views. A smart, consensus-focused leader will build-in time for hearing minority voices, and then, if a consensus doesn't emerge in a reasonable amount of time, the leader calls for group action on the alternative with the best chance of succeeding.

Personal Challenge

Reflect on the way you make difficult decisions, both in your personal and professional lives:

▶ Do you start with clarity of purpose?

▶ Do you generate multiple alternatives?

▸ Do you write down the alternatives?

▸ Do you involve others in clarifying the purpose
  or generating alternatives?

▸ Do you confer with mentors?

Team Challenge

Plan with your team the best way to include more voices in upcoming team decisions. Check first to be sure that you have a clear, shared team purpose. Discuss how more voices—not fewer—can actually help you move faster.

TeamWisdom Applied

Urgent Decisions Are Made at High Velocity Everyday

Mid-September, 1998, my almost-two-year-old son, Thom, underwent emergency surgery for a raging hip-joint infection. The 12 hours preceding the surgery were a study in fast consensus building.

Up all night with acute pain Thom, and his mother, Amy, met Thom's pediatrician at his office as soon as it opened. The doctor suspected that the hip was septic and sent Amy and Thom directly to the hospital where the attending pediatrician took over leadership of the case. With the consent of all departments, this doctor by-passed normal administrative check-in and charting, had Thom assigned to a room, and then rushed him to various departments for lab tests, sonograms, x-rays, an MRI, and nuclear-imaging, followed by surgery. The attending physician's plan was to exploit all available resources to prove the original hypothesis—or find an alternative one fast. Following each test, the attending physician huddled with the technicians who performed the test, the specialists who interpreted it, Thom's mother and myself, and other attendants to pose theories about what was ailing Thom. The septic hip wasn't confirmed until the nuclear imaging, at which point Thom was rushed to surgery to prevent the infection from attacking the hip socket or growth plate.

Don't Rely on a "Common Enemy" for a Sustainable Goal

Instead of simply rallying to beat a "common enemy,"
look for more sustaining and expansive goals that lie
beyond beating an opponent.

Rallying a team to beat a "common enemy" is a frequent and intoxicating business tactic. It is also a cheap trick. What makes it cheap is that results are temporary and they commonly backfire in the end.

Leaders choose "common enemy" strategies because they (1) rapidly point people in a common direction and (2) excite people into action. And, yes, these are two critical measures for determining if your team is "built." However, there can be dire and often unintended consequences for achieving these ends using a "common enemy" tactic. The two largest risks stem from the "us-versus-them" context:

1. Us-versus-them creates impermeable boundaries and halts the information flow in and out of a team. How? The energizing fear of suspicion and paranoia clamps off communication. People evaluate *all others* as either "for us, or against us," so anyone not obviously in the team is assumed to be the enemy. Even loyal team

members who operate on the boundary can become
mistrusted and accused of treason, due to low visibility
within the team.

2. Us-versus-them focuses on a "surrogate" outcome
instead of a genuine achievement. How so? While
win/lose is an intoxicating game, it is possible to beat
a "common enemy" without adding an ounce of value
to your customer or improving your score. Indeed,
"common enemy" strategies often employ unethical
marketing, corporate politics, and even espionage to
facilitate winning. Such tactics elevate the status of
the competitor, making the competitor the "king"
instead of the customer.

Need an example? During the 1970's, Ford, GM, and
Chrysler each had stated missions to "beat the other two."
They then beat on each other while others stole the market out
from under them all. During the 1980's, the semiconductor research and development consortium SEMATECH was created
by the U.S. semiconductor industry to "beat Japan" by regain-
ing lost market share. Then, four years after it declared success,
the consortium continued to wrestle with an unclear identity
while it began exploring a new mission.

Which alignment and empowerment strategies really work?
Leaders with strong TeamWisdom reach beyond "common ene-
mies" for a lasting goal that expands opportunity and wellbeing
at every level of an organization. It's okay to use a "common
enemy" as a launch pad. Then, when you have identified a
common enemy, it's time to ask, "What about this race is so important that we and our competitor(s) are both in it?" Other
questions should occur to you shortly thereafter: "What customer benefits lie beyond the us-versus-them-battle?" And,
"What sustainable team purpose stands on the other side of this
competition?"

If you will reach just a bit farther, your search is sure to uncover a larger and more expansive goal for your team—one which supplies ample direction and energy without the risks of beating out a "common enemy."

Personal Challenge

Reflect on your team experiences. Try to get underneath the hype and determine which of your past experiences was actually fueled by the goal of beating a "common enemy?" List other teams, companies, and communities that exist to beat an enemy. How long have they been in practice? How much longer do you expect them to last until they will need a new "enemy?" What larger goal might give them more power?

Team Challenge

Discuss with your team whether you are unified around beating a common enemy? If so, identify the unintended negative consequences to the team's interaction. Brainstorm goals beyond the "common enemy" tactic. What might be an alternative, unifying goal?

TeamWisdom Quoted

"This past December we set the largest stretch goal for company performance in its history. There were many naysayers—people worried about potential systems issues, competitive actions, insufficient inventory, insufficient people to handle the rush, etc. However, we understood the importance of the goal to hit market share and financial performance targets, as well as benefit from individual incentives and the personal satisfaction that we could get the job done. The company's employees rallied, put together an

> *aggressive plan with many contingencies, and exe-*
> *cuted it flawlessly. December was a big success for the*
> *company and its employees because we climbed a big*
> *mountain together."*
>
> Don Kovalevich, President and CEO,
> Houston Cellular Telephone Company

Reorient the Relationship for Renewed Direction and Energy

When productivity begins to lag, it's a good time to
reorient the relationship.

The change of a calendar year, the end of a fiscal quarter, or the completion of a project phase can all be auspicious times to acknowledge that continued investment is required if work relationships are to continue growing. So can the failure of a critical technology, a change in personnel or budget, or a shift in the scope of a project. When a team crosses one of these thresholds, one of my favorite "maintenance" tools is what I call the Reorientation Process. Assembling all the players for a reorientation is a powerful way to acknowledge that *all* productive relationships go through periods of being highly aligned and in synch as well as periods of being out of alignment.

However, the best time to reorient a team is any time you notice that the sense of shared direction has been lost or that energy has decreased. With practice you will find it isn't difficult to determine when a team has lost its orientation. A team is oriented when everyone has the same understanding of the what, the why, the how and the who of the project. If team members have different ideas about the what, the why, and the how, and the who of the project, you can bet that the team is not operating optimally.

The Reorientation Process is simply a way of getting the team members back on track. To orient or reorient a work team, gather the players together and ask each of them to articulate their views on the following:

► The What. What has the team been formed to do?

► The Why. Why are we here, and more importantly, why are you (the individual team member) here? What is in it for you to be on this team?

► The How. How are we supposed to do the work we were formed to do? What are our team rules and agreements?

► The Who. Who is doing what? What does each of the team members bring to the group in terms of skills and responsibilities?

In my experience, when teams get out of synch, committed members get stuck pushing harder and harder on the content of the team's work. They may not even notice that the team has lost energy and direction. When this happens (and it may happen several times in the life of a team), I like to say "It's always a good time to reorient."

Personal Challenge

Reflect on times when your team has experienced a severe lull or even a breakdown. What precipitated it, an external or internal event? How did your team reorient and move forward again? What would you do differently next time?

Team Challenge

Gather the players together and engage in the Reorientation Process as articulated above. When all team members have been heard, ask the group to craft a clear team goal, one that has meaning for everyone. This will refuel the group so it can accomplish what it was formed to do. You can tell when people are getting back on track because you can see, hear, and feel their energy increase as the direction comes back into focus.

TeamWisdom Applied

Team Reorients Regularly

The Landmark Graphics Corporation Research and Development Directors and the Vice President of Research and Development constitute a team dedicated to managing a 350-member division of a 1600-employee oil and gas, software and services solutions provider. In less than six months, the team missed an important goal, broke some critical intra-team agreements, got a new vice president, and filled a long-vacant director's job. One would expect the group to have descended into chaos, but it didn't. Why?

After each change, the team used its monthly face-to-face meeting to reorient. In particular, the team conducted five critical conversations:

1. To revalidate the task (to choreograph how Landmark ships software).
2. To revisit the interests of the individual participants.
3. To re-negotiate and recommit to team operating agreements.
4. To set aggressive goals.
5. To learn more about the wide range of resources each member brings to the team.

Even when circumstances conspired to cloud the direction of the team, team members left their monthly meeting energized about the future. This is what reorientation can do for a work group.

4

Trusting Just Right

TEAMWISDOM INVITATION

Learning to trust just right can make any relationship better. Although trust is something that is hard to establish and even harder to maintain, it is arguably the most vital resource a company has to draw upon in order to support and sustain long-term working relationships in the new economy. Trust may be the most critical component of global business, for instance.

It's a simple, hard truth. When we are working in teams, no matter how carefully we plan, lack of trust can sabotage our success. Over the course of my career, I have learned that people motivated by accomplishments are the least likely to conceal their agenda, and so, are the most likely to deserve our trust. I tend to trust people motivated by accomplishments more than people motivated by personal ambition.

Experienced leaders can usually tell when people are working on the basis of hidden agendas. But not always. Some people are able to hide their agendas even when those agendas demand that the person work against team goals. Oftentimes, these people believe their agenda is more important than the group's agenda, and their failure to communicate this belief can be devastating to a group's success. When someone has ambitions contrary to the group's goals, the group can't afford to allow that person to participate in a collaborative environment. That person could compromise the environment for everyone.

It's my belief that people who trust freely are those who have established a sense of personal security. Because they are not driven by fear, they are not as worried about getting hurt. They can share rewards, for instance, instead of requiring that all the rewards go to themselves. It's not that these people haven't had their trust violated. People who trust freely and wisely don't build relationships around the exception; they build them around the rule. Most people are trustworthy; most people have integrity; most people want to be a part of a team.

I measure trust by my ability to have what I call "tough conversations" with a person. We all enjoy the feel-good conversations with peers and subordinates in which we praise each other. But working effectively with others requires more than just praising each other. For people to really trust each other, each person needs to know that being able to have "tough conversations" is part of having a good relationship.

Applying the ideas about trust in this chapter will make you both a more trusting and more trustable member of any team, any time, anywhere.

Trust me. This is good stuff.

JOHN W. GIBSON, JR.
Chief Executive Officer
Landmark Graphics Corporation

Trust Reflects Responsibility

As your ability to respond grows, so does your trust in others.

Want more trust in your life? Consider this: We think of trust as something that only happens between particular people for particular reasons. But, if trust exists only between people, how do we explain those all-trusting persons who seem able to trust everybody all the time? Are they naive? Or have they got something figured out? I think they have got something figured out.

From my vantage point, folks who trust everybody all the time have figured out that trust depends on more than interpersonal dynamics: it's also an intra-personal event. Whether we trust others or not actually has less to do with others than it does with our ability to respond to what others do. And this is true not just sometimes, but every time we trust. Trust isn't simply a product of a good relationship between two or more people, it's a product of what's happening inside of you, too.

As you focus on teamwork as an individual skill, you will find the level of trust you are able to achieve in a relationship reflects the level of your individual response-ability. That is, the more you are able to respond to the actions of others, the more you are likely to trust them. As your ability to respond grows, then, your trust in others will grow as well. In the end, how much you trust others is really a reflection of how much you trust yourself.

It might help to explain this complicated observation with a personal example. For three years, I turned down repeated requests to teach Sunday School to toddlers at my church. My justification was "I specialize in teaching adults." The truth was, however, that I didn't trust a roomful of two-year-olds. I didn't know what they would do. I finally admitted the truth to myself and confronted the fear of not knowing what a room full of two-year-olds might do. After I examined the possibilities, however, and came up with a few responses to typical two-year-old behaviors, I was able to go through with the teaching job. As a result of thinking things through, I was able to trust a room full of two-year-olds.

Keep in mind that trust is more about what is inside you than about what is between you and another person. If you are always waiting for other people to prove their trustworthiness to you, maybe, just maybe, you are playing too small a game.

Personal Challenge

Refusing to empower other people is often an example of our imagined inability to respond to what other people might do. Identify at least one relationship where you have been balking at trusting the other party. Consider how you could expand your response-ability in order to trust the other party. Then, take the steps required to do so.

Team Challenge

Discuss with your teammates what it means to trust each other. How will high levels of trust help your team?

TeamWisdom Applied

A Role Model for Trust

Joia Jitahidi is one of our favorite role models for response-ability. A much-loved facilitator who produces extraordinary results when leading Partnerwerks courses, Joia honed her trust skills as founder and principal owner of The Executive Coach, a consulting company in Austin, Texas. Time after time, one-on-one, and in groups large and small, we have seen Joia radiate openness and the willingness to deal with anything that happens! She trusts everyone in her presence completely because there is nothing they can do to which she can't respond productively. How did she get this way? Practice, practice, practice, of course. But what are her practices?

1. Joia is very clear about her values and beliefs. She has explored many different value systems and knows that her choices aren't "right" but are just choices that work for her. This experience makes her not easily threatened when people exhibit different values.
2. She has already confronted what is inside of herself, and so, has such integrity that she cannot be a target for the digs of others.
3. Joia has clearly chosen to use whatever happens as a means to move things forward.
4. She has decided to use her talents to provide the greatest service to the greatest number of people.

The Formula for Building Trust

Making and keeping small agreements is how to begin building trust.

Have you ever been abandoned by a team? Does the fear of this happening again get in the way of your committing to teams?

Team members must have confidence in one another if the team is to be successful. What it takes to build confidence (and, therefore, trust) may seem hard to define, but, basically, the elements are embedded in the way we make and keep agreements. Think about it. Do you trust people who haven't kept their agreements with you? I will bet you don't make important agreements with them anymore.

From my perspective, the formula to build trust looks like this: First, make a small, low-risk agreement with someone, an agreement you can afford to have broken. Second, complete the agreement, keep your end of it, and find out whether or not the other parties keep theirs. Third, make a larger, more risky agreement and repeat the process. This formula sounds really simple, but in my experience it is too seldom applied. Small agreements are easy to make and forget because, obviously enough, they are small. But trust is almost always built by making and keeping small agreements. Why? Because if you don't keep small agreements, you won't get the chance to make large agreements.

Two rules about agreements:

▶ Never make an agreement you don't fully intend to keep (no matter how small).

▶ As discussed in the previous chapter, clean up all broken agreements at the first opportunity. Later in this chapter, I'll tell you how.

Personal Challenge

Carry a 3 × 5 card with you wherever you go and record every agreement you make over the course of a day or two. Carry the card until you complete each and every agreement.

Team Challenge

Establish a shared space or standard communication process for making, completing, and following up on team agreements.

TeamWisdom Quoted

"The only way we can keep so many balls in the air is to have a lot of jugglers and to trust them—not always checking to see whether they're juggling in the right

way. Once we establish a common vision and a shared purpose, I don't want to know what my team members are doing day to day. I trust them."

Thor Ibsen, Vice President, eBusiness Group,
Ford Motor Company[1]

How to Trust Just Right

To optimize the benefits of trusting others,
you actually have to trust a little too much.

Most of us would like to be more trusting. It's just that we have all had relationships where our trust was violated.

One thing is for certain: We can't change other people. But we can change ourselves. So, to be more trusting, the first place to look is at ourselves. Examine how your own trusting goes wrong.

There are only two ways that trust goes wrong: We can trust too much or too little. Unfortunately, as most of us struggle to trust "just right," we usually err in the direction of trusting not too much, but trusting too little. Think about it. In the organizations you know, do people exhibit too much trust or too little?

Here is how I think it works: When I trust too much, it costs me time, money, results, or credibility. Worse, I judge myself and I judge others. That is, I feel like a chump when an agreement is broken because I should have seen it coming. I am embarrassed because I imagine others saw it coming too, and I think I must look like a fool to them. Worst of all, I am apt to maintain a negative attitude toward the person whom I trusted too much.

Most of us work in environments where there is a premium placed on always being "right." In such environments, trusting too much and being burned is seen as a mistake—and making mistakes is seen as being "wrong." There can be dramatic consequences to being "wrong" when the stakes are so high; therefore, the most popular strategy is usually, "At all costs, trust too little."

The immediate repercussions of trusting too little seem never as severe as the repercussions of trusting too much. When we don't trust enough, the evidence seldom appears immediately and seldom is linked to our choices. Just because the evidence is indirectly linked, however, doesn't mean there aren't very real costs to not trusting enough, such as lost opportunities and less-than-optimum team performance. Imagine all the synergies that might have been created if we hadn't peeled ourselves away too soon, then imagine some more. Then imagine more again. That's not even close to what is lost when we don't trust enough.

How can we learn to trust "just right," then, when severe consequences and harsh feedback are the results of trusting too much and minimal, indirect feedback is the result of trusting too little? It's pretty easy, really. Start with small agreements and dare to extend trust beyond your habitual comfort zone. When you follow the formula for building trust described in the previous section, you will seldom—if ever—get over-extended.

Personal Challenge

Examine your current team experiences and identify a situation in which you are withholding trust from your team because you might be shown to be "wrong." Calculate the lost opportunities and other real costs to withholding your trust. With this tangible information in hand, design a different approach. Begin making agreements that give you a chance to practice trusting "just right."

Team Challenge

Discuss with your team what happens when team members trust too much. What happens when they trust too little? What is keeping team members from trusting "just right"?

TeamWisdom Quoted

"Someone who is able to trust freely and wisely is willing to enter into new relationships or situations believing the best about the intents of other people. The trusting person is comfortable making herself vulnerable to the actions of others, even if those actions could do her damage. That's how to create a spiraling of trust."

Andy Robin, Vice President of Marketing, Vantis

Talking about Violations of Trust

When someone leaves you holding the bag, make sure to discuss the causes and effects of the falling out.

If I have persuaded you to try trusting just a little too much in order to trust just right, I can already hear your next question. What am I supposed to do, you ask, on those rare occasions when others do let me down, that is, leave me holding the bag?

The way I see it, the first order of business is a careful assessment of the relationship's value to you. One thing you can do is absorb the violation of trust and chart a new course for the relationship. But there are at least two other choices available to you: You can live with the relationship in its damaged state, or you can remove yourself from the relationship completely. If the relationship is important to you, however, you must engage the people involved in a conversation about the broken agreement. Prepare yourself for such a conversation by studying the seven-step process described below:

Step 1: Acknowledge your own feelings about calling someone on a broken agreement. Doing so is confrontational, and confrontation is only successful when done "cleanly," or, that is to say, done without judgment about the other person. If you are anything like me, you may be feeling fear, doubt, commitment, and courage at such times.

Step 2: Be invited. Conventional wisdom tells us we can't tell other people anything they are not yet ready to hear. Since this is the case, it's our personal responsibility to prepare others to receive our feedback. You can start with something like, "Friend, I want to talk with you about how we are working together. Is this a good time?"

Step 3: Be explicit. Describe the actions that have caused you concern. Be specific in your description of behaviors and deliverables. Tell the individuals who have violated your trust you thought you had an agreement with them for a specific action to take place (by a certain time), and that it appears they didn't follow through.

Step 4: Use cause-and-effect language. Report the consequences to you (and to your team) of the broken agreement. "When you didn't deliver on your promise," you might tell them, "I was unable to complete my task and the entire team's deliverable fell behind schedule."

Step 5: Tell how the broken agreement affected you personally. If you have made judgments about the person—and you probably have—this is the place to say them. Not before. Start with words like, "I assumed . . ." or "I interpreted. . . ." The point is to take responsibility for your judgments and your feelings. You might tell the person, "I decided that your promise is not as important to you as it is to me." You might tell the person, "I felt betrayed."

Step 6: Stop talking and listen. If your words have been compassionate, accurate, and nonjudgmental, you are likely to have tapped into the other person's integrity, and he will be prepared to make amends. If the other person begins blaming or attempting to justify his behavior, simply invite him to examine his own behavior with you.

Step 7: Make a new agreement. Only when you reach this last step is it a good idea to talk about the future. This is the time to tell the other person what you want, how the relationship will be different this time around. You might describe what should happen if trusting becomes difficult. "If you discover you can't keep a promise made to me," you might tell the other person, "I want you to call me the minute you discover it yourself, so we can figure out what to do."

This seven-step process for talking about trust or the lack of trust has been developed out of my own personal experience and years of consulting businesses on how to set up and maintain successful teams. It works for me.

Personal Challenge

It is much easier to practice feedback skills by giving good news instead of bad. Identify someone who has recently kept an important agreement with you or helped you in some other way and initiate a feedback conversation where you work through the seven-step process described above. Make sure to give plenty of positive reinforcement. Then do the same thing in a relationship that could be improved by focusing attention on broken agreements.

Team Challenge

Spend 30–45 minutes in your team giving each other positive feedback. Ensure that every member is comfortable using the seven-step process.

TeamWisdom Applied

Overcoming Distrust through Compassionate Revelation

Five engineering directors in Mega Oil Company (the story is true, but the names have been changed) kept raiding each others' best engineers causing conflict, salary inflation, and diminished productivity for their division. Their boss, whose headcount had been frozen, demanded that they solve the problem amongst themselves. He was careful not to dictate a solution, instead stipulating only that they must share the collective pool of engineers without the conflict of the recent past. To no one's surprise, the subsequent meeting between the five directors began cautiously and progressed slowly, since no one wished to be the first to give anything away to the others. After lunch, they decided to break the ice by taking turns describing and comparing their roles and accountabilities. They hoped this conversation would lead to a plan for how to better distribute the shared talent pool.

When one of the directors, whose name is Arnold, spoke about his roles and accountabilities, the other four soon discovered that he was compensated and managed differently than the rest, and that this difference fueled the rivalry because his interests were not aligned with theirs. The meeting turned on this discovery. The tone of the discussion became lighter as the participants sensed a breakthrough. Arnold had been standing at the flip chart facilitating the meeting. Sensing that Arnold needed to "be taken care of" at that moment, Sharon stood up next to him and announced that she would take over facilitation for this portion of the meeting, and motioned for Arnold to sit down with the others. He did. The group rapidly reached a breakthrough about what they had to do. That breakthrough involved a joint negotiation with their manager to seek equity for Arnold so that they could then collectively manage the head-count issue among themselves.

"Calling" Others on Broken Agreements

Agreements-about-agreements can restore integrity to a relationship.

Do you ever feel compelled (or even forced) to work with people who have let you down by breaking agreements? Do you know what to do when you still desire to operate in a trusting relationship with people who haven't kept their agreements? You will have to "call" them on it (the way an umpire "calls" a foul or a strike). You have to tell them that you noticed they did not keep their agreement and that it is not okay with you. Then ask them to do their part to ensure integrity in your relationship. I call this "making an agreement-about-agreements" and it's the best way I know to responsibly repair broken agreements.

Triage for broken agreements is a three-part formula:

1. Summon your courage and in a direct non-demeaning way, tell the other(s) how important agreements are to you.
2. Ask how important agreements are to them.
3. Make a new agreement together about how you will treat your agreements.

In a team, when you let another person break an agreement and don't call them on it, you are just as responsible for the blow to group performance as the person who let the agreement slide. You can build far greater trust, confidence, and velocity through:

▸ Making only agreements you intend to keep.

▸ Keeping all agreements, no matter how small.

▸ Cleaning up broken agreements when you (inevitably) break them.

▸ Calling yourself and others on broken agreements when they happen.

Personal Challenge

Identify one relationship where the other party has recently broken a small agreement with you. "Call it" in a clear and non-demeaning way and ask for a new understanding about how you will treat each other's agreements in the future.

Team Challenge

Discuss "calling it" in your team and make a team agreement around cleaning up broken agreements. When, where, and how will "calling it" occur?

TeamWisdom Applied

Calling a Broken Agreement

"The company I work for received an unsolicited offer to merge our company into the suitor company. The suitor's CEO assured us that our entire team would remain intact because we were so valuable as a team. We went through extensive due diligence, including having all seven of our senior management team travel to meet with the people of the suitor company. On the second

day of our visit, our CEO quietly left the main confer-
ence room. None of us knew where he went. After about
an hour, I found him in the office of the suitor's CEO.
He explained that he and the suitor's CEO were working through the process of combining the two companies' organizational charts. He stated that it would take
another hour or so, and suggested the rest of us go back
to our hotel (right across the street from the company),
to reconvene after the organizational chart process had
been complete.

When our CEO phoned me an hour later, I called him
on what I described as harmful behavior. I told him I
didn't disagree that the two CEOs should have some
time alone to take a stab at blending the organizational
charts, but that I felt it was wrong to have disappeared
without telling any of the rest of us. We had agreed
before we left home that we were going to stick together
during the visit—his unilateral decision violated that
agreement and had caused me to suffer fear, uncertainty,
and doubt. He answered defensively at first. He wanted
to meet individually with each of us, to show us the
draft organizational chart. I told him that I felt very
strongly we should all review it together. He agreed. We
got together, and the process worked. We very quickly
agreed that the draft organizational chart showed that
there was no feasible way to keep our team together. We
also affirmed our earlier commitment to keep the team
together. The ultimate answer became obvious—we had
to say "no, thank you" to the suitor. Our CEO and I met
with the suitor's CEO the next morning. We spelled out
our reasons for declining the merger offer, and then articulated the reasons the two companies should still

work together on an independent basis. The suitor's CEO agreed. We are now preparing a proposal to work together on a major project. Our CEO thanked me, the next day, for calling him on his behavior."

This story was anonymously submitted
as a response to TeamWisdom Tips.

Clean Up Broken Agreements

Don't sweep your broken agreements under the rug.
Clean them up immediately.

Don't sweep your broken agreements under the rug. Clean them up immediately.

As discussed in previous sections, you build trust by making and keeping incrementally larger agreements. Although most of your relationships will develop positively if you follow the formula, broken agreements do happen, and there is always fallout after the event. What happens if you break an agreement? Your partner can lose confidence in you and may withhold trust. You can avoid this by responding immediately and cleaning up the relationship mess you created.

By applying the following four-step clean-up process, you can resuscitate any relationship:

Step One: Acknowledge you broke the agreement. Make no excuses, simply acknowledge that you blew it. When you are responsible enough to call attention to your mistake, your partner doesn't have to pretend to ignore it, pretend to make it okay, or confront you about it.

Notice that there is a real and valuable difference between explaining and making excuses. Explaining that you did not return someone's call within thirty minutes as promised because your child broke her arm and you were rushing her to the emergency room is an appropriate way to address a broken agreement. Expecting the other party to accept the costs created by this unfortunate circumstance, or explaining all broken agreements with similar stories is another matter.

Step Two: Apologize for breaking the agreement. Tell your partners they didn't deserve to be treated that way by you. (*Hint:* "I apologize to you" often sounds better than "I am sorry.")

Step Three: Ask your partner what you can do to correct the situation. You may know what you need to do to correct a broken agreement, but asking the other party what you can do places the emphasis on repairing the relationship. Besides, it's a chance to make a new agreement and demonstrate trust.

Step Four: Recommit to the relationship. Tell your partner how important the future of your relationship is to you and what you intend to do to ensure that you keep agreements from now on.

Cleaning up broken agreements is vital to maintaining a productive working relationship with your partners. The four-step process just described is so important that the last four sections of this chapter are devoted to examining each step in greater detail.

Personal Challenge

Think of at least one relatively minor broken agreement (such as forgetting to call someone back) and one relatively major broken agreement (. . . yes, that one) and clean them both up before the end of the week.

Team Challenge

Ask your teammates what agreements you have broken and ignored, rather than cleaned up. Use the four-step clean-up process to set things right.

TeamWisdom Quoted

"Trust begins here. It's not like we're in an industry where there's an accepted business model. We're in an industry where everyone has to listen to and learn from each other every day. You can't build community in cyberspace if you don't build community in your workplace."

Mary Furlong, Founder and CEO, Multimedia Gulch[2]

Acknowledge Mistakes

Acknowledge relationship mistakes quickly and move to resolution.

The first step of the four-step process for cleaning up broken agreements is to acknowledge that you made a mistake. It's simple enough, once you have decided to take the ego hit. Without acknowledgment, however, you won't be able to move the relationship forward to resolution. For this reason, acknowledgment is actually more important than apology.

Think of how upsetting it is to you when other people don't acknowledge their errors. If it happens too many times or if it goes on for too long, it can feel like they are refusing to acknowledge your existence. How frequently do you cause these kinds of problems yourself? How long do you go on denying before you recognize your mistake? This is the kind of behavior that can cause you and your organization lost productivity. When we refuse to acknowledge mistakes, we get to stay stuck—no learning, no moving forward, no gain, only loss.

How you acknowledge a relationship mistake makes a big difference. Be careful about the language you use, and make sure the other party knows you are sincere. Here are some different phrases you can try:

- ▶ I blew it.
- ▶ I made a mistake.
- ▶ I let you down.
- ▶ I screwed up.
- ▶ I said I would do something and I didn't.
- ▶ I failed to keep an agreement.

Personal Challenge

Recognize where you have made a mistake in a relationship. Acknowledge it now. Pay attention to what happens.

Team Challenge

Mistakes are bound to happen, they are inherent to the learning process. Talk with your teammates about how to admit and accept mistakes. Make agreements about how admitting and accepting mistakes should be accomplished within the group.

TeamWisdom Applied

My favorite illustration of the power of acknowledgment is a story about Herb Kelleher, chairman of Southwest Airlines. After Southwest rolled out a new "Just Plane Smart" advertising campaign in 1992, they learned that the slogan already belonged to a small airline maintenance company in South Carolina named Stevens Aviation. Other powerful executives might have chosen to ignore, fight, or crush the tiny company on whose toes they were stepping. Not Kelleher. He acknowledged quickly that he and Southwest had infringed on Stevens. Ultimately, a highly publicized mock arm-wrestling match was held between Kelleher and the Stevens Aviation chairman. The Stevens chairman won the match and then promptly announced that the world was big enough for both Stevens and Southwest, giving Southwest permission to use the slogan.

By resolving the problem in such a creative way, the two companies generated free publicity for themselves worth fifteen to twenty times their combined annual advertising budgets. The moral of the story for me is that resolution flows from acknowledgment—and can be accompanied by huge gains.

TeamWisdom Quoted

"Teams at SEI have maximum freedom to experiment— but clear responsibility to disclose when an experiment doesn't work. Bad news is like fish. The older it gets, the worse it smells."

Richard Lieb, Senior Executive, SEI[3]

Apologize Effectively

A successful apology signals responsibility and learning, not subordination or shame.

The second step of the four-step process for cleaning up broken agreements and other relationship mistakes is to apologize. Do you know how to apologize so the person you are apologizing to will get it the first time? Apologize so you are done and both you and the other party are ready to move to resolution? From my observation, not many of us do.

Most of us apologize with an attitude. We are either reluctant or overly humble. The reluctant apologizer frequently can't help being sarcastic and might say something like this: "What? Are you waiting for me to say something? Oh, all right then, I'm s-o-o-r-r-y. Do you feel better now?" The overly humble apologizer frequently exhibits shame and might say something like this: "I'm sorry, it was my fault. I should've known better. If you give me another chance, I'll try to do better. . . ."

The trouble with both of these situations is that they mask the critical issue of responsibility, instead of highlighting it. If the other party also needs to be right—requiring us to grovel and blame ourselves—unskilled apology can seem to make a situation worse instead of better.

People with TeamWisdom apologize readily, with grace, and with integrity, because their apologies come from intentions of responsibility and contrition, not from reluctance or shame. A responsible apology might sound like this: "You didn't deserve what you got from me." Or, "I learned a lesson and am ready to demonstrate my growth in this relationship." Skilled apologies hit their mark immediately. You know when you have received one.

What's the secret of getting others to get it? As in many of the thorny problems discussed in this book, the secret is for you to get it first—and then signal that you have. We can only apologize from a position of responsibility when we have first processed our own errors and truly feel the other party received less than our best treatment.

When you get it, in other words, others will be hard-pressed to miss it.

Personal Challenge

The next time you are in a position to apologize for a mistake you made, instead of chanting the same old, "I'm sorry," try this instead: "I apologize to you. You didn't deserve that from me." Make sure you hold your head high and look the other person in the eye with confidence.

Team Challenge

Discuss with your teammates how you can best hear apologies from each other. Include words, phrases, tones, and actions that really demonstrate ownership and responsibility.

TeamWisdom Quoted

"Trust. To me, trust is one of the essentials for learning. Wherever you have a trusting environment, you have a much more productive, much more humane organization."

Chris Turner, Xerox Business Services, Learning Person[4]

How to Make Amends

To get back to normal following a relationship mistake,
ask how you can make amends.

The third step in the four-step process for cleaning up broken agreements and other relationship mistakes is to ask the offended party what you can do to make amends. Once I have acknowledged my mistake and apologized for it, you might be thinking, why should I ask how to make amends? Maybe you are thinking this might open the door for the other party to demand the most damaging penance. Hopefully not. In my experience, when my intention to make amends is clear, others don't feel the need to shame me.

The best reason to ask the offended party how you can make amends is to obtain the target information that can get the relationship back on track, back to a place where you can resume building trust. Here are three practices people with TeamWisdom use when they are in the midst of cleaning up relationship mistakes:

1. Don't assume you know what to do to get the relationship back into exchange. As responsible and introspective as you may be, it's impossible to fully predict how the offended party is interpreting your broken agreement or relationship mistake. Besides, if you just mind read, you will miss an important opportunity to hear the other person's request. Make a new agreement and keep it.

2. Avoid making amends in a way that encourages the offended party to say something like, "Oh, that's okay. Don't worry about it." This could be perceived as attempting to slip off the hook. For example, if you borrowed and then broke or lost something of value, make sure the other person knows you are fully prepared to replace it before asking if that will make amends.

3. When others do try to penalize or shame you, don't accept their response! Remember, you can negotiate the level of exchange in any relationship. You do it all the time. If the other party is unreasonable, you can always decide the relationship is not so important to you as your own integrity. Don't let irresponsible people attempt to take advantage of your openness.

Personal Challenge

Choose a relationship that needs mending. Depending on the situation, try out one of these statements on the other party once you have acknowledged and apologized for your part in a relationship mistake:

- ► How can I make amends?
- ► How can I make it right with you?
- ► How can I correct the mistake?
- ► What can I do to make amends?
- ► What will make it right with you?
- ► What can I do to correct the mistake?
- ► Is there any way I can make amends?
- ► Is there a way I can make it right with you?
- ► Is there a way I can correct the mistake?

Team Challenge

With your teammates, scan your collective interactions and results to date. Ask yourselves if you have made mistakes or broken agreements with customers, other teams, or managers. How can these broken agreements be mended?

TeamWisdom Applied

Cleaning Up Well Can Produce Surprising Results

One Sunday afternoon, John Cook, an amazing instructor who has led courses all over the United States as well Australia, Canada, Kuala Lampur, and Singapore, left Austin on a plane trip that was to deposit him at Westchester County, NY. John was to conduct a three-day Partnerwerks seminar in Westchester County starting Monday morning. Sunday night, my home telephone rang. It was John calling from Chicago where his connecting flight had just landed—about five and a half hours late! The flight had stayed on the ground in Austin for hours due to weather and air traffic control directions from O'Hare. All flights for the rest of the night to the East Coast had been canceled due to the same weather that had closed the airport.

Obviously, John was not going to make it to New York to start the course the next morning. By the time I hung up the phone, John and I had come up with the following plan. John would arrange a flight to New York for the next morning in case the customer wanted to go ahead and start the class a day late. Then he would find an airport hotel and get a few hours of sleep. I would call our customer's voice-mail and explain that there would be no facilitator in the classroom the next morning as expected.

The next day, our client met the class and invited them to return on Tuesday morning. John flew to LaGuardia Airport and drove the 90 minutes to Westchester where he met with the client to confirm the go-ahead for the next day. The next morning he discussed with the participants what they wanted. He was willing to stay for three days, but less than half the class could rearrange their calendars on such little notice. With a bit of creative redesign and with a good deal of input from the participants, he conducted a two-day course instead of the usual three-day course.

Afterwards, I called our customer to apologize for not delivering the service that they had purchased, and,

I offered to bill the customer only for Partnerwerks' direct costs, and to charge no course fee. To my surprise, the customer refused my offer and insisted on paying for the entire three-day course. He said that he would not hold us accountable for the weather delay, and that in his eyes, John had already demonstrated responsibility and commitment in redesigning the event on the fly for a great two-day learning experience. The customer told me that they would expect the invoice in the full contracted amount and would be ordering more courses soon!

How to Recommit after Making Amends

*After making amends for a relationship mistake,
recommit by describing how the relationship will
work better in the future.*

The fourth and final step of the four-step process for cleaning up broken agreements and other relationship mistakes is to recommit to the relationship. Do this by telling the other party (who has already received your acknowledgment, apology, and negotiated amends) exactly how you intend to treat the relationship in the future.

What does this do? Well, if you are sincere in making this recommitment you will reduce the likelihood of repeating the past mistakes, or mistakes similar to them. Recommitment also allows your partners to restore their faith in you. Remember, the end result of the clean-up process is to continue to build trust. When you voluntarily recommit to a relationship, you start over with a blank slate. Make sure there isn't any residual bad feelings so that your new dealings with the individual can proceed with trust unencumbered by the past.

I would also recommend that your recommitment be stated out loud. When recommitment is stated out loud, the new standard for your own behavior becomes public, and you declare a willingness to be held to that standard by other people. Such public commitment is irrevocable. An expectation of responsibility is imbedded in your public statement, and everyone knows that every effort is going to be made.

So, recommit to your partners and signal you have "raised the bar" for how you intend to attend to the relationship.

Personal Challenge

Focus for ten minutes on a mistake you never want to make again. Scan your behavior to date. Have you acknowledged your mistake, apologized, and attempted to make amends? Yes? Great! Now finish the clean up. Tell the other party aloud what you will do to care for the relationship from now on.

If you want to make your new attitude really stick, tell the other party in the presence of teammates. This simple step will virtually guarantee you will never make the same mistake again!

Team Challenge

Acknowledge, apologize, make amends, and recommit. Discuss with your team the value of each of the four steps.

TeamWisdom Quoted

"To survive those downtimes, you have to understand what real teamwork is—keeping promises, keeping commitments. Not everyone understood this, but both Knight and Prefontaine did, because that's what

Bowerman taught his athletes. As one of our first employees said, " 'Not everyone grew up on the track with Bowerman. They didn't understand what it took to be great.' "

Nelson Farris, Director of Corporate Education, Nike[5]

5

The Collaborative Mindset

TEAMWISDOM INVITATION

Soon after joining Human Code, I found that the company culture had been damaged. Employee and executive morale was low. Communication was poor. Looking for support and direction, we subscribed to TeamWisdom Tips and used the weekly issues as a point of discussion for our meetings. This taught us a new way of management, focusing on shared purpose, team effort, and trust combined with personal responsibility. TeamWisdom Tips helped all executives build stronger interpersonal skills. We now experience almost zero attrition, very high morale, substantially increased productivity, and significantly improved financial results. (To subscribe to TeamWisdom Tips, send a blank email to TeamWisdom-On@partnerwerks.com, or visit www.partnerwerks.com.

Our vision of the workplace at Human Code is of a scaleable design studio—creative communities of artists, poets, and engineers. In the ideally collaborative culture, employees all hold themselves accountable for successfully completing commitments. All hold shared accountability for success when teams are involved. Blame, politics, and envy do not creep in because employees have high mutual regard for each other and because any conflict that does arise is handled with fair process. We each make honest, authentic commitments to others and to the community. We are frank with ourselves and with each other and avoid commitments that we can not or will not fulfill. If a relationship breakdown occurs, we are of high enough integrity to identify the breakdown and do what it takes to repair the relationship.

Human Code makes hiring decisions based first on character, second on core competencies, and third on skills. What are the characteristics of people with a collaborative mindset?

► People with a collaborative mindset stay focused on long-term goals while being sympathetic to the individual needs and goals of participants.

► They demonstrate a strong ability to step into another person's shoes and understand the world from that person's point of view.

► They can strongly support another person's agenda without losing sight of the overall mission.

► They maintain a strong sense of personal power and integrity—caring for themselves and never losing their backbone.

To sum up, people with a collaborative mindset are responsible. Being responsible means you have the vision to imagine a successful outcome, the wisdom (knowledge, skills, and experience) to be able to respond, and the motivation (desire and energy) to insure that the outcome is positive for everyone.

> Please study and enjoy this book on TeamWisdom. It keeps us mindful of what is most important to businesses in the new millennium: people and relationships.
>
> ED PERRY
> President and CEO
> Human Code (recently purchased by Sapient)

Play a "Big" Game Instead of a "Small" One

Expanding the boundaries of your game will provide opportunities and make people want to play on your team.

Are you willing to be completely responsible?

- ► for yourself?
- ► for your family?
- ► for a process, team, or department?
- ► for the entire company?
- ► for a church or community effort or project?
- ► for a neighborhood or city?
- ► for a state?
- ► for a nation?
- ► for the world?

Collaborators are inclusive players. They see themselves as responsible to and for themselves and also to and for the people with which they work. To become truly inclusive players requires us to expand our circles of reference, our playing fields, or what we might call our life "games."

People who boast they are "only out for Number One" exclude a big chunk of the world from their lives. Interestingly, most of these people seem to struggle with friends, spouses, managers, and coworkers who they think "are out to get them." When I have an opportunity to coach such people, I sometimes ask them: "Is there any chance you have been defining your life as too small a game? What would it look like for you to define a larger life game?"

Being invited to answer these questions often helps people see where and how they have been maintaining boundaries that keep their worlds small. It is only a small step from that awareness to seeing how they can play the game of life at any level they choose. This can be tremendously freeing. Here's the secret: The larger the game you define for yourself, the more opportunities will be available and the more teammates you will engender.

How does this philosophy play itself out in the real world, you might be asking. Here's an example: When a team leader who has narrowed her focus to include only her team's success widens this focus to include the entire company's success, other teams (against whom the team has been competing for resources) become potential partners instead of roadblocks. Of course, a leader can always restrict her responsibility to just her team. If she chooses to be responsible to all company teams, however, her success can extend over a much wider field.

Think about how large a work game you can define for yourself. At the same time ask yourself this question: Am I ready for a larger life game? How would you need to shift your boundaries to afford yourself and your teams even wider opportunities for success?

Personal Challenge

Draw a circle on a piece of paper and write inside it everything for which you are willing to be completely responsible.

Outside of the circle, write down everything you see yourself either ignoring or struggling against. Quietly consider what you have written. Think about how expanding your boundaries (including more items inside the circle) will allow you to get more out of life, or, in other words, play a larger life game.

Team Challenge

Discuss with your team how you can expand the boundaries of your task, the problem, or your resources in order to play a larger game.

TeamWisdom Applied

Perhaps the Biggest Game Ever Played!

"In 1927, at age thirty-two, finding myself a 'throwaway' in the business world, I sought to use myself as my scientific 'guinea pig' (my most objectively considered research 'subject') in a lifelong experiment designed to discover what—if anything—a healthy young male human of average size, experience, and capability with an economically dependent wife and newborn child, starting without capital or any kind of wealth, cash savings, account moneys, credit, or university degree, could effectively do that could not be done by great nations or great private enterprise to lastingly improve the physical protection and support of all human lives, at the same time removing undesirable restraints and improving individual initiatives of any and all aboard our planet Earth."

R. Buckminster Fuller[1]

The TeamWisdom Theory of Relativity

Treat whatever people tell you as true for them.

Some people exhibit such a need to be right that they can't stand evidence to the contrary. These are the folks who work overtime to prove others wrong and who disparage anyone who espouses a different point of view. People who adopt this attitude make team communication difficult because it turns most discussions into debates of right versus wrong. (Do you realize the word "discussion" has the same root as "percussion" and "concussion"? The root comes from the Latin "quatere" which means to shake. "Discuss," then, actually means to shake apart!)

People with TeamWisdom listen completely and respectfully to speakers who represent different views. Why? Because they know that "right" and "wrong" are always relative, because they are evaluative. People with TeamWisdom don't fear different points of view: They know different points of view offer opportunities to build and to expand. They know different points of view will not threaten them with extinction.

Consider this. What is considered "right" in your family may well be considered "wrong" in another person's family. This is true for your department as well, not to mention your culture, classroom, book, market, organization, religion, nation, and on and on. Judgments of right and wrong always emanate from a particular point of view, based on a set of values, beliefs, and attitudes. And values, beliefs, and attitudes are always relative.

Take for example the relationship between marketing practitioners and design practitioners. The activities of marketing departments and design departments emanate from very different points of view. Sometimes, it can be quite difficult for marketing practitioners and design practitioners to work together. But marketing would have nothing to sell without design. And design would have no niche for its products without marketing. In fact, each is only part of a bigger picture in the information economy, each domain requiring input from the other for successful completion.

To adopt the TeamWisdom theory of relativity, consider all of your knowledge, ideas, and opinions as functions of your unique perspective or point of view. Consider other people's knowledge, ideas, and opinions as functions of their points of view. All are valid and true. Some are more applicable than others in certain circumstances, but all are equally valid and true from their relative positions. The fun part of life (and of practicing TeamWisdom) comes from integrating your point of view with as many other points of view as you can. To do this, though, you have to be willing to hear and validate other people's opinions. And, not just when you agree with them. All the time.

Personal Challenge

Remove "right" and "wrong" from your vocabulary. Replace them with "works" and "doesn't work"—as in "that works for me" and "that doesn't work from my point of view." Try it for three days and see if you can feel your TeamWisdom growing.

Team Challenge

Ask your teammates to consider removing "right" and "wrong" from their vocabularies, at least within the team. Encourage people who resist to consider their reasons carefully and share them with the group.

TeamWisdom Quoted

"One of the main problems when young, inexperienced leaders—including myself once—deal with conflicts is that they often stubbornly think they are right. They may well be right from their point of view, but their solution may not always be the best solution for the organization."

Olli-Pekka Juhantila, Manager, Outsourcing,
Nokia Mobile Phones

Honor Differences

Treat diversity as a functional challenge,
not a political or moral issue.

At this moment in Western history, we are experiencing an unparalleled explosion of diversity and strong political and moral support for sustaining it. U.S. employment laws and most religions mandate that all people deserve equal rights and access to opportunities. To reap the full benefits of diversity, however, organizations have to do more than simply comply with employment laws. Despite the difficulty of including persons with unfamiliar habits, customs, lexicons, and vocal inflections, people with TeamWisdom understand the benefits of doing so, not just to the people with these unfamiliar habits, but to themselves.

Of course, it takes considerable effort to understand people from different cultures and to help them understand us. When others operate with different perceptual filters and from different contextual frames, the interests, opinions, and needs of people from different cultures are likely to be different from our own. In such circumstances, it is sometimes deceptively easy to exclude them from decision making.

As lateral-thinking guru Edward de Bono teaches, however, to arrive at high quality ideas, we need lots of ideas to choose from. Different ideas. Most often, the best ideas appear after we have considered something from several different points of view. (De Bono calls this "lateral" thinking.) Now, if we overlay this principle of lateral thinking onto the explosion of diversity in the workplace, it becomes easier to see one of the primary benefits of diversity. From which team then would one expect the best ideas to emerge—a team of similar people or a team of diverse people?

I thought you would say that.

People with strong TeamWisdom treat diversity as a functional imperative, not a political or moral issue. Those who agree with this point of view will actually amplify the contributions of other people and ignore differences that have nothing to do with the focus of their work. The people with the greatest potential to contribute to the team, the people best able to integrate their ideas into the ideas of the team, are the people who require the least conformity—except to the purpose, relationships, and processes of the team. Everything else can and should vary for the highest quality to emerge.

Personal Challenge

The next time you encounter people from different cultures think about how you are treating them. Do you treat them like you "should," keeping in mind the unwritten rules of political correctness? Or, do you treat them keeping in mind that they have different points of view, which could add texture and depth to your life, goals, and outcomes?

Team Challenge

With your teammates, examine the ways in which the team requires members to conform to the team's purposes and practices. How does this conformity limit potential contributions? Where can you loosen up so the team can derive real benefit from diversity?

TeamWisdom Applied

Significant Benefits from Honoring Differences

In mid-1990, six months before Partnerwerks was conceived, I was employed at Technology Futures, the firm that led to the realization of Partnerwerks itself. I had just sold a client on our ability to design and deliver great teamwork training and had enlisted the people who later became my two co-founders to help design the three-day learning event now known as Being Powerful in Any Team (for more information, please go to www.BeingPowerful.com).

We were three very different people. Larry Browning is the ultimate professor. Extremely well-read and with a photographic memory for research literature, Larry's focus during our design efforts was on the theoretical integrity of our information. Debra France was a former advertising executive with a strong interest in adult learning processes. This interest led her to become a practitioner of neuro-linguistic programming (NLP), and not surprisingly Debra was inclined to look at things from the learner's perspective. I, on the other hand, was inclined to look at things from the customer's perspective. Every bit of my attention was devoted to making sure that the customer's interests were met.

At first, Larry, Debra, and I experienced a lot of conflict about how to design the event. It was Debra who noticed that we were each very consistent in the positions we took during these conflicts. She suggested that we examine those "voices," name them, and agree to honor them. Larry's became the voice of theory, Debra's was the voice of interaction, and mine was the voice of structure. This way of identifying our different perspectives was such a breakthrough that the next day I bought all of us bright red sweatshirts with the names of our voices embroidered in gold letters. Soon, we began referring to each other as Mr. Theory, Ms. Interaction, and Mr. Structure. The course design turned out great because it honored all three voices.

Oh, and ten years later, I still have my sweatshirt!

Competitor or Antagonist?

Distinguish between antagonism and competitiveness when you are sizing up the competition and figuring out how to inspire your team.

Which is the better strategy: cooperation or competition? Look out, it's a trick question.

People can be motivated through cooperation or competition, and both have the potential of adding value to a team's work. Cooperation supports synergy while competition fosters invention and choice. They can both be useful forces in group relationships. The trouble comes when we think of cooperation and competition as mutually exclusive. It's politically correct these days to deem competition "bad" or destructive and cooperation "good" and constructive. Neither force, however, can exist without the other.

How is it that common opinion has come to sheath competition in negativity and controversy? Well, my associates and I have observed that business people are prone to mislabeling certain types of business behavior "competitive" when they are not. In fact, these types of behaviors are actually "antagonistic," a term which needs to be distinguished from "competitive." Failing to maintain the distinction between antagonistic and competitive can weigh heavily on the performance and spirit of team members.

I once had a teacher who told me how he had demanded of himself that he graduate with the highest grade-point average in his college class. He accomplished this task, in part, by identifying his closest competitors, discovering what courses they were taking, and checking out of the library all the books they would need to succeed. That's antagonistic behavior, not competitive behavior.

Most of the world class competitors that I have observed think of the word "competitive" as meaning something like "striving together with others." One likely source of this specific usage is the Latin "competere," which means "to strive together." Somewhere in the development of the general usage of the word, however—maybe because we have used war as a metaphor for business in the Western world—"competitive" has taken on a meaning closer to "striving to eliminate." Every day I hear people in business speak of competitors with disdain, sarcasm, contempt, and cynicism. Coworkers chuckle and deem this an exercise of "the old competitive spirit." From my viewpoint, however, such behavior demonstrates antagonism, not competition. And, in my experience, antagonism is incapable of producing the kind of sustainable, high performance actually needed to compete successfully in the marketplace.

I have heard executives deliver impassioned motivational speeches about how they hate the competition. Yet when I ask those same employers how many of them would want to work for an organization that advertises antagonism as a core value, no one raises a hand. If you think about it, expressing contempt for a competitor whose goals are similar to your own denigrates your own goals. My teacher realized this upon winning the grade-point title. After he told us his story he admitted that he was embarrassed and disgusted by his hurtful tactics. Vowing to dedicate himself to personal behavior that honored himself and his competitors, he went on to build a business, amass a personal fortune, and then found a business school to teach entrepreneurs how to play "above the line" and win.

Competitors with TeamWisdom respect, revere, admire, honor, and even love their competition. Try it. It's a good place to make your stand in business.

Personal Challenge

Reflect on the state of mind you call your "competitive spirit." Can you distinguish it from antagonism? Identify and explore the distinctions. These distinctions may be subtle, but spending some time thinking about them can make you a more powerful team player.

Team Challenge

Begin a team discussion by asking these questions: Who are our internal and external competitors? What is our attitude toward them? How can we shift our attitudes and behaviors to respect, revere, admire, and honor our competitors?

TeamWisdom Applied

Competitors Grow Through Collaboration

The passing of movie critic Gene Siskel offers a poignant lesson in the dynamic relationship between competition and collaboration. Reporting on Siskel's death for the *Chicago Tribune,* Rick Kogan noted that Siskel and partner, Roger Ebert, had once been arch rivals working for different Chicago papers. Kogan wrote: "Their rivalry was intense, during the 70's the two critics barely spoke. '. . . We intensely disliked each other,' Siskel recalled. 'We considered each other a threat to the other's well being.'" Even though they were rivals the two were paired by a TV producer in 1975 and, together, they transformed the practice of movie criticism. Of course, they also gained celebrity status and fame.

What's the point? Well, first, this rivalry-turned-partnership illustrates the way that competition and collaboration give rise to each other. Second, and herein lies the learning, our greatest opportunity for creative breakthrough and abundant reward often awaits our willingness to approach our greatest threat. In Siskel and Ebert's case, this meant collaborating with an arch rival.

What could you accomplish if you joined forces with your greatest threat?

Intentional and Reactive Relationship Outcomes

Identify relationship values that transcend win/win, win/lose, and lose/lose. Then establish an acceptable range of outcomes for every relationship.

Last section, I invited you to reexamine the traditional view that cooperation and competition are mutually exclusive states. I suggested we view them as occurring simultaneously in every relationship. If cooperation and competition are not opposites, then, what are they?

The way I would suggest you view interpersonal dynamics, the opposite of competition is martyrdom. That's right. Martyrdom describes the set of interpersonal dynamics wherein one person loses so another can win—a lose/win situation. If martyrdom is the opposite of competition, what do you think is the opposite of cooperation? The answer is mutual harm. Think about it. If cooperation results in win/win, then the opposite must be lose/lose—and that is mutual harm.

Figure 5.1 and Table 5.1 place the relationships I have been discussing on a spectrum. The vectors describe the various value orientations possible in a specific relationship at a specific time.

So, what can this model teach us about TeamWisdom? Among other things, it illuminates the following truths:

▶ We don't have to choose between cooperation and competition. We have many more choices in any relationship than to "either" cooperate or compete.

▶ People behave based on their conscious intentions and their unconscious reactions. The relationship between their conscious intentions and unconscious reactions makes up a behavioral range. The value orientations listed in Figure 5.1 can be understood as if they represented the various stops on the face of a clock. A person may intend to operate only between twelve o'clock and three o'clock, for instance, or exit the relationship (altruism, cooperation, and individualism). Under stress, however, this person's subconscious needs may stretch her behavioral range from eleven o'clock to

Figure 5.1. The Spectrum of Possible Value Orientations

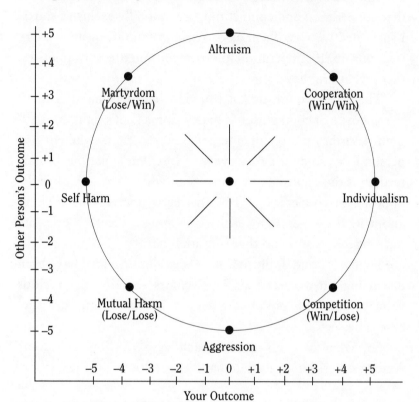

Table 5.1. The Spectrum of Possible Value Orientations

Your Value Orientation	Your Outcome / Other's Outcome
Altruism	0 / Win
Cooperation	Win / Win
Individualism	Win / 0
Competition	Win / Lose
Aggression	0 / Lose
Mutual Harm	Lose / Lose
Self Harm	Lose / 0
Martyrdom	Lose / Win

six o'clock. Another person's range might span from one o'clock to five o'clock or from three o'clock to six o'clock. When this person feels threatened in a relationship, he may extend this range to include seven o'clock (mutual harm) in an effort to avoid allowing another person to win at his expense.

▸ People differ in their abilities to perceive and to own their behavior as opposed to blaming them on circumstance or an antagonist.

People with TeamWisdom consciously choose their value orientations and outcomes in every possible relationship. And they strive to correct their behavior rapidly when they feel themselves reacting outside their range instead of choosing within it.[2] How about you?

Personal Challenge

Consider your important work relationships and use Figure 5.1 and Table 5.1 to identify your behavioral range within those relationships. Now identify your "reactive" range—the range that identifies your value orientations when you feel yourself under threat. Are the two ranges different? What can you do to bring the two ranges into better correspondence?

Team Challenge

Discuss Figure 5.1 and Table 5.1 above with your team. Do they help you represent and track typical behaviors? What are those behaviors? What do you want them to be?

TeamWisdom Applied

Anyone who has ever had a rival will appreciate this story. Once upon a time, there were two merchants located on the same street. Each was afraid that the other was out to put her out of business. This distrust led to a price war where the two competitors took turns slashing prices. At the same time, they began an advertising war and each of the merchants spent ever-increasing amounts of money to promote her wares. Of course the eventual result of this escalation was a dramatic weakening of both businesses. It was completely lose-lose since neither business could make any profit by operating with no margin and a huge advertising budget. Finally, one of the merchants relented and actually raised her prices a little because she decided to quit reacting to her competitor and simply do what she had to do to run her business. Two things happened. She made a little money, and more importantly, her competitor raised her prices a little and reduced the advertising barrage. Each party continued this intentional de-escalation until the system reached equilibrium and each of the merchants had plenty of business and plenty of margin to make a decent living.

Value Both the Task and the People Performing the Task

To break through conflicts, apply this dual-value mindset: The task must get done, and the people involved must have an extraordinary experience.

One of the most powerful, simple, and unique teambuilding tools in my arsenal is actually a mindset. This mindset is powerful enough to create breakthrough communication and thinking. Although easy to cultivate, few people have it—or know they have it. It's so simple it took me a long time to realize I had it—and how useful it can be.

This tool, this mindset, is actually a commitment to a specific belief about people and work. The belief creates an intense "resolve" that, when activated, summons courage, quells doubt, and dramatically influences communication between teammates. The opportunity to use this tool shows up sooner or later in every team, especially when pressures begin to build.

Ready to know what it is? Believe you can do the following two things at the same time: Value the task, and value the people performing the task.

While working to accomplish a task, conflict can arise between accomplishing the task and treating people humanely. When this conflict does arise, most people throw their weight behind one side or the other. Either the task gets done at the expense of treating someone badly, or people are treated well at the expense of the task getting done. Maybe this small, almost invisible, mindset is the reason so many people in the corporate world feel they have to "lose" so that the organization can win? Leaders with a technical, task-based inclination are famous for sacrificing people's feelings in the name of completing the task. Leaders with a people-based inclination are equally famous for sacrificing completion of the task in the name of "humane" relationships. The simple, yet extremely powerful, Team-Wisdom mindset is to favor neither of these two orientations over the other.

Don't subordinate one orientation to the other. Instead, value both equally! People with TeamWisdom resolve to accomplish the task and to make sure everyone has a great experience while doing it.

Personal Challenge

Focus on your most recent exposure to extraordinary team performance. Examine it for evidence of the dual-orientation mindset described above. Can you see where this mindset started? How it spread? Was the mindset consciously discussed or did people just assume, "We can accomplish the task and not hurt anyone!"

Next focus on your most recent exposure to less-than-extraordinary team performance. Where in the process did team members make the unnecessary assumption that you have to choose between the task and treating people well? How could you have corrected the situation and reestablished a course aimed at total success?

Team Challenge

Discuss with your team the assumptions you hold about achieving results. Do different members of the team value completing the task over treating people well? How can you work together to establish a dual-orientation mindset? Resolve to do it.

TeamWisdom Applied

"Trust Efficiencies" Produce High Performance

The development team at DTM (Desk Top Manufacturing Corporation, NASDAQ: DTMC) was really under the gun, and team members didn't like it one bit. Due to market shifts and unfortunate timing, DTM decided it had a nine-month window to build what should typically take from 12 to 15 months. To make matters worse, the development team consisted of people from hardware, software, and support groups who had no history working together and came with different tolerances for risk and ambiguity. The cobbled-together group met and, after voicing concerns, decided to commit to the task. One of the team tools they adopted was a set of agreements designed to speed up the working relationship. Perhaps the group's smartest move was posting the agreements for everyone to see on a flip-chart front and center in their meeting room. In the early days of the project, this visual reminder worked well because everyone noticed when anyone violated an agreement! Team members frequently and compassionately called one another on violations such as evaluating someone's new idea or failing to communicate early warning of a pending risk. The team members' behaviors sharpened to the point of extremely high performance, and the team exceeded project goals and company expectations. They attributed their extraordinary success to "trust efficiencies" that were gained from team behavior. They truly valued both the task and the people.

Keys to Extraordinary Collaboration

Extraordinary Collaboration = Exchange + Expansion + Integrity.

As discussed in an earlier section, competition and collaboration are complimentary forces occurring at the same time. For example, I might play a game with my boys where I encourage them to outdo dad on a given task in order to win my attention. This may (and often does) spur them to scheme, or collaborate, together to beat me at my game. In the business realm, as the world's markets become increasingly available, our businesses are exposed to more and more competition. As we experience more competitive forces, we tend to look harder and harder for collaborators to help us absorb and respond to the competitive shocks. Simply stated, competition and collaboration cause each other.

While this is a fascinating concept to contemplate in the abstract, we can see competition and collaboration at work in our everyday lives, as people, departments, and organizations strive to attract, rely on, and assist new "partners." Here are three keys to producing extraordinary collaborations:

1. Get in *exchange*. We cannot have ongoing collaborations if our relationships are out of exchange. Exchange is the foundation for all business relationships. In fact, social exchange theorists offer a powerful argument that exchange is the basis for all relationships. In other words, we take turns granting favors, taking risks, talking and listening, giving and receiving, back-scratching, etc. I've observed in the workplace that the cornerstone of collaboration is positioning one's relationships so that each party is providing value and receiving value and perceives that the relationship is fair in that regard. If the relationship is not considered to be in exchange by each party, collaboration attempts will fail.

2. Apply the power of *expansion*. Create a bright future for the relationship by developing a system-wide goal that (1) is bigger than any of the parties to the collaboration, (2) requires that all parties achieve this goal equally, and (3) promises much larger rewards (or exchanges) for the participants.

3. Build *integrity* into the relationship. Pursuing expansion is risky because investments and rewards may not always be in one-to-one correspondence. For example, to build expansion with a partner, I might need to make heavy internal investments and/or adjustments. And then the partner still could defect. In other words, there may be opportunities for either dishonesty or distrust to break the collaboration and the relationship. (I've seen more

breakdowns occur from distrust than from actual dishonesty.) To build integrity into the relationship follow these four steps:

▶ Communicate very frequently.

▶ Tell the truth.

▶ Make and keep agreements about membership in the collaboration.

▶ Create a conflict-resolution process by talking in advance about what you will do to maintain exchange, expansion, and integrity if something goes wrong.

Exchange, expansion, and integrity will each be further developed in the next three sections of this chapter.

Personal Challenge

Scan your critical relationships for exchange, expansion, and integrity to determine how the three keys are affecting your performance in those relationships. Choose one relationship in which you can pinpoint an opportunity to use one or more of these keys to shift the relationship from ordinary to extraordinary. Then, do what it takes to open the door to that new vista.

Team Challenge

Discuss with your team how you can apply these three keys to move team results from ordinary to extraordinary.

TeamWisdom Quoted

"This restaurant is about creating something bigger than any of us could accomplish alone."

Michael Schlow, co-owner and chef of Radius Restaurant[3]

The Bedrock of Collaboration

"Contractual" exchange is a necessary, but insufficient,
condition for collaboration. For rock-solid collaboration,
practice "relational" exchange too.

In the last section we examined the three keys to extraordinary collaboration: exchange, expansion, and integrity. Remember, we can't successfully collaborate until we are "in exchange." To be "in exchange," each party to a relationship must be providing and receiving fair value—as each perceives it.

Concerning the issue of exchange, my associates and I have noticed that people with TeamWisdom (and companies that collaborate well) make two powerful distinctions in determining who to approach for collaboration.

Distinction # 1. Being in contractual exchange does not necessarily constitute "partnering," but many people act as if it does. As a consequence of the total quality movement, many people and companies developed the habit of referring to all their business associates as "partners." Because sometimes this is hyperbole, the term "partnering" doesn't carry much weight in many business circles today. When we use the term "partner" to designate people with whom we are considering doing business, it's important to make sure that it refers to business practices that encourage and support expansion and integrity. It's a good idea to develop the habit of examining your "partnerships" for signs of expansion and integrity.

Distinction #2. How we treat one another in the business relationship can support or threaten the continuation of the contractual exchange; therefore, it's critical to make a distinction between contractual exchange and relational exchange. A relationship is in exchange when each party perceives that he is being treated fairly by the other party. Even a relationship that is in contractual exchange may be too costly to maintain due to reasons outside the contractual agreements. If you are like most people I talk to, you have probably quit one or more valuable contractual exchanges because of their relational costs to you. Relationships drop out of exchange when one party does something unexpected and/or unfair to another party. Examples include back-stabbing, niggling after the deal is made, asking too many favors, consistently ignoring needs, and breaking agreements.

What should you look for? People with TeamWisdom know that staying in relational exchange requires that they keep the following two principles in mind: First, you must remain sensitive to and learn from others' relationship requirements (those requirements that go beyond contractual values); and second, you must keep communication channels open so that any party can suggest an adjustment to the agreement at any time.

Making the distinction between contractual exchange and relational exchange is critical to high-level collaboration. If you don't think this distinction is important, I encourage you to recall the last time you got a signal that "the deal's the deal" from the other party in a relationship, and also got the signal that the other party wasn't willing to take any responsibility for the relationship beyond the contractual exchange. How much effort did you put into the work? And how large was your profit?

Personal Challenge

Choose one relationship you consider to be an ongoing collaboration or partnership. Define the contractual exchange (i.e., what you are giving and receiving). Then, examine how you and your partners successfully keep the relational aspects of the exchange in balance. Go beyond noticing how nice, open, and flexible each of you are. Describe how each of you takes responsibility for the relationship, how you communicate about that, and how you make adjustments.

Team Challenge

Discuss with your teammates the contractual exchange guiding the actions of the team. Then examine how each team member remains in relational exchange. Notice where adjustments need to be made and make them.

TeamWisdom Applied

"I once took over an Army ROTC program on a campus that also had an Air Force ROTC program. The two organizations had historically acted in competition with each other since resources (and recruits) were a scarce commodity. In other words, they operated through authority or economic power (as I understand the concepts of Kenneth Building). I decided that we needed to act in a more TeamWisdom fashion, however, and move to a "power with" relationship. So I started sharing my personnel. In one area in particular, marketing, we started including Air Force literature at our recruiting tables and started sending prospects who had an interest in aviation to the Air Force. It just so happened that the headquarters for both programs were in some shabby trailers. Individually, both programs had been trying to move into better facilities for years. As we developed our "power with" relationship more and more, we formed a fairly effective lobbying group and were able to get into new facilities. I am convinced this would not have happened had we not acted in a TeamWisdom fashion."

Ed "Drive On" Hampton
(ehampton@mail.ucf.edu)

Expansion Is the Collaborative Leader's Most Powerful Tool

Expansion creates collaborative opportunities.

An entrepreneur friend of mine has built and sold eight companies. He is now beginning a massive economic development project that requires the simultaneous launching of three or four different companies with a large number of different kinds of partners. As my friend told me about his plans recently, I found myself leaning farther and farther back in my chair as if to place him and what he was saying in a larger context. Finally, I raised my gaze over his head to take in the sky in my effort to create a space large enough to "contain" the enormity of his vision.

I was so impressed with the size of his "game" that I asked him, "How is it you think so big?" He answered, "I have to think that big to have a chance to create anything worthwhile." When I asked how he planned to keep the game manageable, he replied that he didn't plan to manage it. He believes firmly that after he has clarified the opportunity properly and attracted talented people, all he has to do is hold tightly to his own role and hang on.

What a difference there is between managing and leading! Managers have been taught to envision things they can control. Managers operate, thereby, in a realm of self-limited resources. Leaders, on the other hand, out of a dedication to their vision, create opportunities that can attract an unlimited number of voluntary followers and resources. Collaborative leaders create expansive opportunities for partners.

Expansion, the second key to collaboration, is the most powerful tool available to any leader. Don't be afraid to set a large goal, even a huge goal, one that will require many collaborators to achieve.

Here are some guidelines for generating expansion:

- ► An expansive goal is larger than any one participant can achieve by herself. If it were not, it wouldn't demand collaborators.

- ► The more expansive the goal, the more opportunity will be created. Some teams never turn away new-comers because they see every newcomer as extending the opportunity.

- ► The greatest opportunities for expansion often arise from what appear to be the most threatening circum-stances.

- ► Expansive goals are usually so clear and specific that they require little if any verification. (Example: President Kennedy's challenge to put a man on the moon by the end of the 60's.)

- ► Expansive goals are usually so bold that participants don't immediately recognize how the goals will be met. Such goals afford collaborators a sense of urgency. (Example: When Kennedy set the goal mentioned above, the state-of-the-art in rocketry, according to some NASA scientists I once interviewed, was that they were pretty sure they could launch a rocket from Cape Canaveral and have it hit the ocean!)

- ► Expanding a goal is one of the best ways to integrate different people's views. At the same time, integrating people's views is one of the best ways to expand a goal.

Personal Challenge

What opportunity could you tackle with one or more other people that could create a greater opportunity for all of you?

Team Challenge

Evoke expansion in a group gathering (a meeting, committee, family outing, lunch group, etc.) by posing this question: "What could we pursue together that would create a highly attractive opportunity for all of us?" As the conversation develops, apply the guidelines above. Watch yourself raise the collaborative energy in the group. Expansion is a powerful force!

TeamWisdom Quoted

"Pioneers in any endeavor have no maps to study, no guidebooks to read, no pictures to view. Those in previous centuries who set out in search of new lands were often not very realistic: their boats were small, provisions meager. But the lack of realism didn't deter them from making the journey; in fact, it helped. Their dreams of what was possible fueled their enthusiasm and better enabled them to persuade others that many interests would be served."

James Kouzes and Barry Posner,
The Leadership Challenge[4]

Relationship Integrity Makes Collaboration Possible

Whatever else you do, don't be the first to defect.

The last two sections have deconstructed extraordinary collaboration. Examining the formula "Extraordinary Collaboration = Exchange + Expansion + Integrity," we have established exchange as the "bedrock" and expansion as the "wellspring" of great partnerships. Now it's time to look at the critical element of integrity.

Integrity is one of those words that is hard to define. People working in different fields understand the term differently. The definition of integrity I like best comes from the field of structural engineering (After all, relationships are structures, aren't they?). As Buckminster Fuller put it:

> Integrity is the ability of a system to maintain shape under pressure.

I like this definition because it has a benevolent cultural neutrality to it. It stands at once inside and outside all moral, ethical, and religious beliefs.

As we apply this definition of integrity to human collaboration, we understand the "system" simply as the relationship between people. What kinds of pressures typically cause relationship systems to lose their shape? A relationship system is put under pressure when one party places his interests before the collaboration, leaving the others hanging. Another kind of pressure occurs when parties conclude that other parties aren't trustworthy. This distrust can cause them to defect on the other party in the relationship.

Shakespeare fans may recall Othello's dilemma: Trust can never be proven, but distrust is the source of its own proof. (For those of you who have forgotten the story: When Iago tempts Othello to see his beloved Desdemona as disloyal, Othello begins selectively filtering information. Eventually, he convinces himself she is disloyal, kills her, and then discovers she has always been loyal. In his grief, he kills himself.) In the volatile arena of human relationships, trust is a fragile creature. It requires sanctuary—and continual sanction—to survive.

The best way to ensure trust is to hold onto relationship integrity with all your might. Don't give in to pressures to give it up. If exchange and expansion are in place in a relationship, integrity is all that's needed to produce an extraordinary collaboration. If integrity is in place too, relationships can withstand pressure exerted on any of the other various parts. Here are four practices to buttress integrity in relationships:

1. Develop your collaboration deliberately and communicate very frequently to affirm your interdependence, to update information, and to maintain rapport.

2. Always communicate what's true for you, so suspicion never has a chance to arise.

3. Make and keep agreements about participation in the collaboration. Pay close attention to alignment, so trust can build.

4. Create a conflict resolution process by planning in advance what you will do to maintain exchange, expansion, and integrity when something goes wrong. This process gives everyone something to hold onto when pressures make things feel uncertain.

Once you have mastered these four practices, you can use this shortcut to 100-percent relationship integrity: Never be the first to defect.

Think about it. Even small defections, like breaking a small agreement, or gossiping about a team member, can begin to erode confidence in the relationship. Once confidence has been undermined the door is open for distrust and defection.

To gain a reputation as someone who can always be trusted in a relationship, then, never defect first! Does this mean you have to become a doormat? No. Instead, as soon as you feel the need to put yourself before the collaboration (and there is never anything wrong with needing to do this), tell on yourself! In other words, take your discomfort as a signal that you should consult with the other team members, so you can negotiate a change in the relationship together.

As Buckminster Fuller also said, "Unity is plural and a minimum of two." This is always, always true in teams.

Personal Challenge

Make a mental survey of current partnerships and consider one that could stand some reinforcement. Create more of a sense of sanctuary by promising to the other team members that you will never, ever defect on them. Ask them to do the same with you. In other words, tell each other out loud that if any of you ever needs to take care of your own needs before the needs of the collaboration, you will talk with each other immediately about your feelings and needs.

Team Challenge

Review the four practices that buttress integrity in relationships. Discuss with your team how you will employ the practices in times of stress. Consider making an oral agreement never to defect on one another.

TeamWisdom Quoted

"There is something metaphysical about taking a concept, making it a reality, and creating a great enterprise. The management of any startup is the administration of the unforeseen. . . . Bureaucracy is a state of mind, and it's remarkable how quickly that state of mind can be created."

Lou Dobbs, Founder, Space.com[5]

Integrate for Expansion: Expand for Integration

The largest purpose integrates all perspectives and expands to fulfill all needs.

People with TeamWisdom looking to live and work "on" purpose know the relationship between integration and expansion: integrate to expand, and expand to integrate.

Integrating and expanding in the context of relationships can be explained in terms of how bodies relate to each other in the physical universe.

Gravity and radiation are complimentary forces that operate on all matter in the universe. Gravity is an integrating force that pulls things together, toward a center. Radiation is an expanding force that pushes things outward, away from the source body in all directions so that it ultimately intersects (and often combines) with the radiation of other bodies. For example, it's the intersection of the sun's gravity with the earth's gravity that keeps the earth in orbit around the sun. And the sun's radiation provides life energy to earth. In this instance, integration and expansion create a complimentary relationship dynamic.

Integration and expansion operate similarly among people. Consider the metaphor for a moment, and you will see that there is some truth to this comparison.

When we live our lives "on" purpose, we radiate an essence of that purpose—like the sun radiates heat and light. The purpose we radiate connects everything we do. It's easy to see, generally speaking, that certain people trust you immediately because they experience life energy and confidence in the essence you radiate. Similarly, when we live our lives "on" purpose, we are likely to be continuously scanning for people capable of assisting us in that purpose, and our "gravity" attracts them to us and integrates them into our lives.

To apply these dynamics consciously, people with Team-Wisdom practice the following:

> ► "Integrate in order to expand" as a way to draw people
> towards each other and hold them there until two or

more points of view mesh into a larger, more expansive whole.

▶ "Expand in order to integrate" by suspending judgment and looking beyond preconceptions for the purpose of defining a vision or a "game" large enough to include or integrate people previously not included.

Personal Challenge

Harness the complimentary forces of integration and expansion to help you discover or name your purpose. Take 10 minutes to inventory who "orbits" around you and around whom you "orbit." Then, articulate in simple terms what has drawn these people together. This reflection holds critical clues to your purpose.

Team Challenge

Review together the team's purpose. Address these questions: How can we further integrate our ideas, points of view, and skills to expand our frame as a team? How can we expand our frame of reference, our team perspective, to integrate different people or ideas?

TeamWisdom Quoted

"At Radian, I met with the vice presidents in my nationwide organization weekly by teleconference. We also assembled in one room three times per year and did three days work in two long days. We addressed the issues that everyone thought were most important and worked them to an intermediate or final solution, as appropriate. We worked until we were worn out, but we laughed a lot too. Since people were tired, they said exactly what they thought. After

one of these meetings, one of our long-term vice presidents said to me, 'I love my job . . . everyone who sits around our table would do anything possible to help me with any problem I have. If something should happen to you, any one of us could fill in, and that person would be successful because we would all work to ensure that he or she was.'"

Dr. Neal W. Kocurek, Co-Founder, Radian International

Conclusion: Demonstrating TeamWisdom from This Point Forward

CONGRATULATIONS! If you have read this book all the way through to the conclusion, I assume you are a dedicated learner who is keenly interested in TeamWisdom. You deserve to be congratulated. I appreciate your interest and thank you for your diligence.

My challenge now is to assist you in demonstrating Team-Wisdom in all of your work relationships from this point forward. I say "demonstrate" because what you do is far more important than what you know, remember, or tell to others. Why? Others judge you by what you do, not by what you know or say. When we judge ourselves, on the other hand, we tend to give ourselves the benefit of the doubt. We judge ourselves by our intentions, not our actions. So demonstration is most important in relationships. And demonstration is the only way to display the integrity of what you say and what you do.

So it is one thing to consider TeamWisdom intellectually. It is quite another to internalize it and consistently apply Team-Wisdom to your relationships. I know many smart people who are intellectual wizards. They have earned high grades and multiple degrees, but they don't seem interested or able to apply what they say they know. They pontificate, but they don't demonstrate.

175

To demonstrate what one knows takes more than intellectual smarts, it requires experiential smarts as well—what one might even call "street smarts." What I mean is that true learning results from a combination of theory plus experience. By "theory" I mean ideas, concepts, and models about how things work. For instance, this book is full of theories about TeamWisdom, but reading and understanding these theories alone is not enough to provide you with TeamWisdom. By "experience" I mean that one must apply theories to one's own life situations in order to truly know how they work and how to work them.

When pondering how best to practice the ideas in this book, keep the following simple equation in mind: Theory + Experience = Learning.

Choose to Demonstrate TeamWisdom

To make use of what you have learned, you must choose to demonstrate TeamWisdom in all of your relationships. Ask yourself the following question to determine if you are ready to choose this course of action:

Am I willing to do my very best to demonstrate Team-Wisdom in all of my relationships at work?

Then listen for your internal response. At this point, you probably already know the answer.

If your answer is "no," then I thank you for reading this book and considering the invitation to demonstrate TeamWisdom. I trust that in the future you may consider TeamWisdom as a viable option for your work relationships. If your answer is "yes," the rest of this chapter is intended for you.

Commit to the Journey

If you answered "yes" to the above question, you are now at the beginning of an extraordinary journey of discovery, learning, and rewards. As you now know, your learning is not complete just because you have almost finished reading the book. You start a new level of learning with your attempts to apply what you have read. As you well know from a life of trying new ideas, sometimes good ideas mesh well right away with the rest of your behavior and sometimes they don't. For instance, consider learning to walk. It took you days or weeks, maybe even months, to learn to walk, even though it was a relatively simple idea. You saw lots of other children who had all the same equipment that you had doing it, yet you just didn't have the strength and coordination to walk when you first chose to. But you didn't quit trying! The idea that you could do it was very strong with you.

When you believe that a theory (model, idea, concept, principle) is valuable, but don't see immediately how to demonstrate it, there will be a period of awkwardness and even mistakes while you attempt to apply the idea. You will attempt to put the idea into action and you will receive feedback about what works for you and what does not. This feedback is critically important. Buckminster Fuller once said that "Every time man makes a new experiment he always learns more. He cannot learn less." You have demonstrated that principle in every part of your life so far, from walking to relationship building. The next step to demonstrating TeamWisdom is to get on with it.

A Five-Step Action Plan

There are many ways to incorporate the ideas in this book into your work life. The following five-step action plan is my suggestion for how to get started.

Step One: Assume personal responsibility for team productivity. At your next opportunity, whether in individual informal encounters or at a team meeting, announce to team members that you will only do work that leads to the entire team's success. Furthermore, announce that you will not be able to meet your goals unless the team meets its goals, so it is in your best interest for the team to be extremely productive and effective. Finally, tell your teammates how you have decided to do everything in your power to help the team gel and operate at superior levels of performance.

Step Two: Get in the same boat together. At the next meeting, ask teammates to put aside individual roles and have a conversation about what you will collectively accomplish. For a moment, think of the team as a single unit, indivisible into smaller units, and answer this question: "What must this unit do?" Insist on continuing this conversation until everyone seems to share the same clarity about what the team has been formed to do. After the function of the team has been established, make that task focus your "super-objective" and give it more importance than any other objective or goal.

Step Three: Determine "What's in it for me?" and then "What's in it for you?" Once you know your super-objective, sit down at your keyboard or with pen and paper and generate a series of answers to this question: "What is in it for me to pursue this task, assignment, or super-objective?" Keep asking the question and writing down answers. Encourage yourself to probe deeper and generate more possibilities. When you have a complete list (five to ten answers), prioritize your responses until you truly understand your motivation for serving on the team. After you know what's in it for you, begin to ask your teammates the same question. Ask them "What's in it for you to pursue this task with this team?" Then wait patiently for responses. Encourage their answers and help them determine which answers seem most important or energizing. Watch for nonverbal cues like sudden smiling, twinkling eyes, head rocking back, or a gaze of recognition. These nonverbal cues can tell you when teammates have accessed an important desire. Test for the most important interests by asking the question "Is that important to you?" and listening for a congruent and powerful "Yes!" You can also test for commitment by asking them the following question: "If by serving in this team, we can help you get (fill in their important interest), then would that be worth your investment in this team?" I bet you the price you paid for this book, that they will say "Yes!"

Step Four: Make and keep agreements. Since you have made your interests known, wouldn't you like to protect them? While at your keyboard or sitting with pencil and paper, inventory your "shoulds." These are the expectations you have about how others "should" behave in your presence, in your teams, or at meetings you attend. List them all. Most people have "shoulds" about who, what, when, where, how, and why to communicate. Many variables determine communication: timeliness, confidentiality, participation, honesty, openness, respect, and more. Once you have your list, prioritize it in terms of which expectations, if actually turned into operating agreements, would gain the most productivity for you and the group. Then figure out how and when to ask your teammates to make agreements that will cause your most important expectations to come true. One of Partnerwerks' associates, Sue Begeman, took a job once that included a peer worker who was reputed to be very difficult to work with. Sue did the exercise that I recommend here, then took this woman to lunch so they could get to know each other. Near the end of the lunch, Sue made this statement: "I want you to know that I will never defect on you. That means that I will never complain about you or undermine you behind your back. I will always be direct with you. In fact, I will do everything that I can to be on your side, and if I can't, you will be the first to know so that we can decide together how to deal with it. Would you be willing to make the same pledge to me?" The peer worker did. Sue never had a problem with this person and enjoyed an excellent collaboration.

Step Five: "Call it!" By this time you know how to craft the foundational elements for TeamWisdom. But they are fragile and must be protected. While the agreements are still fresh, ask others if they will help you "call" each other on behavior that is inconsistent with the team's task, team members' interests, and your stated agreements. They will most likely say, "Yes." That is the easy part. Actually keeping to your agreements is not so easy. Next, tune your antennae to recognize all actions by yourself or your teammates that are inconsistent with the foundation you have created. When you recognize inconsistent behavior in yourself or others—and you will—immediately "call it" in a manner that allows the behavior to be examined and corrected. For instance, if you find yourself blaming someone for a unfortunate position that you are in, stop. Acknowledge that you were just "laying blame" by framing it that way. Say "I think I was just laying blame on Richard, and that certainly doesn't make me more resourceful. A more responsible way to view it would have been to see that I allowed myself and Richard to get into a situation where I would resent Richard if he didn't come through in just a certain way." After telling it like it is, take steps to correct the situation.

Own Your Results

There are two valuable tools that can support you at every step of your TeamWisdom journey. The first is the Responsibility Chart that appears on page 11. If you take 100-percent responsibility for the quality and productivity of every relationship at work, then you will be truly committing yourself to the path of discovery. This means forgiving rather than shaming yourself when relationships don't work, refusing to blame unproductive relationships solely on others' behavior, and eliminating excuses about why it is okay to stay in an unproductive relationship without attending to it.

The second tool is an extremely important feedback principle that will assist you in staying on the TeamWisdom path. Please commit this to memory:

True communication is the response you get.

This phrase might need some explanation in order to make complete sense. It is based on the idea that no communication attempt initiated by you is complete until you observe the effect of that communication on its target. Once you observe the response, then you know if your communication achieved your intent. Said another way, we don't know what communication has been received by our target until we see the response.

The value of following this principle is that you will become increasingly aware of your intentions, how you demonstrate those intentions, and how your demonstration is received. This awareness will help you discover what works and what doesn't. If you are following this principle, you will increasingly become more aware of your intentions in every relationship and every communication, and you will own the responses that you get.

Associate with People Who Expect TeamWisdom

Your journey will move more swiftly and successfully if you surround yourself with people who expect you to demonstrate TeamWisdom. There are a variety of ways you can do this:

▸ Make a list of all the people with whom you work. Divide the list into two groups, those who demonstrate TeamWisdom and those who do not. I know that the dividing line separating the two groups can appear somewhat arbitrary, but I bet you will have no trouble creating two lists. This will help you to understand who will welcome and encourage TeamWisdom and who will present the most challenge (as well as the most need!).

- ▶ Initiate projects with colleagues who demonstrate TeamWisdom. Make agreements to support each other in a high-responsibility relationship. These relationships will be simultaneously safe and challenging. They are safe because you trust each other's intentions. They are challenging because you have such high expectations for each other's behavior. You will find tremendous opportunities to learn from each other.

- ▶ If you have not already done so, go to www.partnerwerks.com and subscribe to TeamWisdom Tips so that we can support you each week.

- ▶ Place yourself in situations where TeamWisdom must be developed and practiced. These include teams and collaborations, even task forces and committees. They do not have to be at work. Some of the most challenging opportunities exist in community and church activities.

- ▶ Download the free TeamWisdom Leader's Guide from www.partnerwerks.com and let it help you make decisions about how to build teams in which you serve.

- ▶ Attend Being Powerful in Any Team (www.beingpowerful.com).

Take Baby Steps

The universe of TeamWisdom skills and behaviors is large and can seem overwhelming. If that is the case, here is what you should do. Select just one TeamWisdom skill or behavior that appeals to you and that you wish to apply. Now, think about the opportunities to practice this skill that are presented by your work relationships. Apply this formula:

- ▶ When you demonstrate TeamWisdom in that situation, acknowledge yourself for meeting your intentions.

▸ When you don't demonstrate TeamWisdom in that situation, catch yourself, then forgive yourself. Correct your behavior if you still have a chance.

▸ Commit to catching yourself sooner, forgiving yourself faster, and correcting more successfully.

A great TeamWisdom teacher once taught me that anything worth doing is worth doing poorly. It is far better to commit to fumbling one's way up the learning curve than to avoid any chance of making a mistake.

I wish you a world of productive relationships at work.

Notes

Introduction

1 I first saw the Responsibility Chart in a seminar titled "Money and You," and for the last ten years I have studied the implications of the chart with Bill McCarly of Austin, Texas. For more information on "Money and You" visit www.excellerated.com.

2 Tom Peters, *The Project 50 (Reinventing Work): 50 Ways to Transform Every Task into a Project That Matters,* Alfred Knopf Publishers, 1999.

Chapter One

1 If you need help resisting "group-think," please read the excellent book by Jerry Harvey, *The Abilene Paradox,* Lexington Books, 1988. And then, if you want to know more, try Harvey's newest book *How Come Every Time I Get Stabbed in the Back My Fingerprints Are on the Knife?* Jossey-Bass, 1999.

2 "The Leader of the Future," *Fast Company,* June 1999, Issue 25, p. 130.

3 "Xtreme Teams," *Fast Company,* Nov. 1999, Issue 29, p. 310.

4 Marsha Sinetar, *To Build the Life You Want, Create the Work You Love,* St. Martin's Press, 1996.

Chapter Two

1 Thomas Nef, *Lessons from the Top: The Search for America's Best Business Leaders,* Doubleday, 1999.

2 Robert K. Greenleaf, *Servant Leadership: A Journey into the Nature of Legitimate Power and Greatness,* Paulist Press, 1983.

3 "The Secrets of Their Success," *Fast Company*, June 1997, Issue 9, p. 67.

4 "The Secrets of Their Success," *Fast Company*, June 1997, Issue 9, p. 67.

5 If you are interested in more detail on Axelrod's research in reciprocal altruism, read *The Evolution of Cooperation*, Basic Books, 1985 or *The Complexity of Cooperation*, Princeton University Press, 1997.

6 "Whole Foods Is All Team," *Fast Company*, Issue 2, April 1996, p. 103.

7 "Xtreme Teams," *Fast Company*, Issue 29, Nov. 1999, p. 310.

Chapter Three

1 "It Takes Two," *Fast Company*, Nov. 1998, Issue 19, p. 212.

2 "The Secrets of Their Success," *Fast Company*, June 1997, Issue 9, p. 67.

3 "Whole Foods Is All Teams," *Fast Company*, April 1996, Issue 2, p. 103.

4 "Make Smarter Mistakes," *Fast Company*, Oct. 1997, Issue 11, p. 152.

Chapter Four

1 "Collision Course," *Fast Company*, Feb. 2000, Issue 31, p. 118.

2 "Third Age—Do You Belong?" *Fast Company*, Aug. 1998, Issue 16, p. 162.

3 "Total Teamwork," *Fast Company*, June 1998, Issue 15, p. 130.

4 *Fast Company*, Oct. 1996, Issue 5, p. 113.

5 "The Nike Story: Just Tell It," *Fast Company*, Jan/Feb. 2000, Issue 31, p. 44.

Chapter Five

1 R. Buckminster Fuller, *Critical Path*, St. Martin's Press, 1981, p. 124.

2 The model and chart are adapted from C. G. McClintock and E. V. Avermaet, "Social values and rules of fairness: A theoretical perspective." In V.J. Derlega and J. Grzelak (Eds.) *Cooperation and Helping Behavior Theories and Research*, Academic Press, 1982.

3 "Their Specialty: Teamwork," *Fast Company*, Jan./Feb. 2000, Issue 31, p. 54.

4 James Kouzes and Barry Posner, *The Leadership Challenge*, Jossey-Bass, 1995.

5 "Starting Your Startup," *Fast Company*, Jan./Feb. 2000, Issue 31, p. 81.

Index

About Partnerwerks

PARTNERWERKS provides responsibility-based team skills development to professionals worldwide. We bring collaborative practices and performance support into highly competitive business environments so you get more done better and faster. Our approach recognizes that high performance comes from responsible individuals working together in supportive environments. Partnerwerks applies industry best practices and Christopher Avery's research to support you in achieving outstanding business results.

Download a Free Leader's Guide

Get help using this book with groups. Download a free leader's guide from www.partnerwerks.com.

Register for a TeamWisdom Public Learning Event at www.beingpowerful.com

Sign up for "Being Powerful in Any Team." Develop strategies for accomplishing extraordinary things with others. Attend yourself or bring your team.

Subscribe Free to TeamWisdom Tips

Send a blank email to TeamWisdom-on@partnerwerks.com and receive provocative and fun tips and challenges every week.

Dig Deeper and Learn More at Partnerwerks Online Library

Loads of articles, a FAQ on teams and leadership, and links to team information at www.partnerwerks.com.

Get Complete Information on the Range of Services We Offer at www.partnerwerks.com

On-site learning events: Develop collaborative competencies in your workgroup.

Talks and presentations: Let us help you inspire participants in corporate events.

Change: Lean on us as you transform your organization with collaboration strategies.

Team and meeting facilitation: Achieve shared direction and energy fast.

Executive coaching: Gain clarity quickly and move forward confidently.

Partnerwerks

P.O. Box 28160

Austin, TX 78755

PHONE (512) 342-9970

FAX (512) 342-9975

info@partnerwerks.com

www.partnerwerks.com

About the Authors

CHRISTOPHER M. AVERY

cavery@partnerwerks.com

Husband, father, learner, eagle scout, and president of Partnerwerks, Christopher M. Avery, Ph.D. continuously searches for the most effective means of working together. As a business advisor, Avery remains very concerned with the underlying win/lose design philosophy for work in organizations. His mission is to add to business's bottom line through the application of collaborative practice for people in competitive environments. A sampling of his clients includes 3M, AMD, Charles Schwab & Company Electronic Brokerage, Exxon, IBM, Motorola, Nokia, TV Guide Interactive, and Wells Fargo Bank.

Each year Avery speaks at dozens of corporate meetings around the globe inspiring people to breakthroughs that advance their work and personal relationships. As a result of Partnerwerks' accelerated learning programs designed by Christopher and his colleagues, thousands of scientists, engineers, professionals, and executives in scores of companies have dramatically improved their ability to get more done with peers.

Over one hundred of his articles on trust-building, achieving rapid consensus, leading people who don't report to you, motivating peers, and collaborating under competitive conditions have been published in academic and trade journals, news-letters, and magazines. Subscribers around the world read TeamWisdom Tips, his digital weekly. Avery also writes a monthly column for the 3M Meeting Network (www.3m.com/meetingnetwork).

For his doctoral research Avery studied technology transfer at MCC, the first major R&D consortium, and earned his Ph.D. in the Communication of Technology from The University of Texas at Austin. That research is reported in *The Journal of Technology Transfer,* and in *Technology Transfer in Consortia & Strategic Alliances* edited by David Gibson and Raymond Smilor.

Avery occasionally teaches at The University of Texas at Austin. He serves the exciting new economy in Austin as "co-dean" of Leadership for the Austin Software Council University. He cherishes living in Austin with Amy, Jake, and Thom who together enjoy bicycling, trips to beaches, and sailing.

MERI AARON WALKER
btl@swbell.net

Meri Aaron Walker is a proven communication strategist with a passion for human collaboration, technology, and entre-prenurism. Based in Austin, Texas, since 1991, her firm, Between the Lines, helps businesses locate their most powerful communication channels and then build two-way messaging mechanisms that link them with critical audiences. Clients include Fortune 500 firms, non-profits, education, and a host of small to medium-sized technology companies. With over 30 years in business communication and production in every conceivable medium, Meri's greatest pleasure comes from finding new ways to collaborate that optimize group creativity. She completed her M.A. in Communication at the University of Texas at Austin.

ERIN O'TOOLE MURPHY
Erin@partnerwerks.com

Erin O'Toole Murphy is an organization designer. Her passion is crafting learning events and organizations that lead to highly effective collaborative action. Erin has trained Sony management in Japan, led human resource teams, and designed corporate training initiatives. A perennial team catalyst, Erin was a scholar-athlete on a nationally-ranked collegiate field hockey team and a co-leader of a transcontinental bicycle ride. She now uses her skills and creativity to consult, coach, and train others. She holds a B.A. from Northwestern University and an M.A. in Whole Systems Design from Antioch University. Erin lives in Austin, Texas, with her husband, Gerry.

TeamWisdom Invitation Contributors

SUSAN INGRAHAM ASHLEY

As Vice President of Human Resources for Houston Cellular Telephone Company, the leading wireless provider in Houston (one of the largest wireless markets in the country), Susan Ashley has substantial experience building a high-responsibility, operationally-excellent work culture while serving on an executive team that has successfully navigated wave after wave of new technology and competition.

OLLI-PEKKA JUHANTILA

As Manager of Outsourcing for Nokia Mobile Phones, the world's leading manufacturer of cellular telephones, Olli-Pekka Juhantila has substantial experience designing and implementing powerful partnering practices across an extensive supply chain spanning Europe, Asia, and the Americas.

MICHAEL S. OSWALD, JD

As Vice President, General Counsel, and Chief Administrative Officer of NowDocs.Com, the world's leading provider of distributed printing and same-day delivery for documents that are too urgent for overnight delivery, Michael Oswald blends the perspectives of an astute contract attorney with those of a partnering and quality expert resulting in extraordinary synergies for NowDocs as it creates a world-wide business.

JOHN W. GIBSON, JR.

As CEO of Landmark Graphics Corporation, a global software solutions provider of over 1600 employees serving the world-wide oil and gas industry, John Gibson has substantial experience with the impact of trust on sales, product development, and operations management. He is also very familiar with developing one-on-one working relationships across continents and cultures.

ED PERRY

As President and CEO of Human Code, the award-winning premier digital content studio with offices in Austin, the San Francisco Bay Area, and Japan, Ed Perry has substantial experience managing the culture of a creative shop while at the same time designing a scaleable business model, managing growth, and preparing for an initial public offering.

Berrett-Koehler Publishers

BERRETT-KOEHLER is an independent publisher of books, periodicals, and other publications at the leading edge of new thinking and innovative practice on work, business, management, leadership, stewardship, career development, human resources, entrepreneurship, and global sustainability.

Since the company's founding in 1992, we have been committed to supporting the movement toward a more enlightened world of work by publishing books, periodicals, and other publications that help us to integrate our values with our work and work lives, and to create more humane and effective organizations.

We have chosen to focus on the areas of work, business, and organizations, because these are central elements in many people's lives today. Furthermore, the work world is going through tumultuous changes, from the decline of job security to the rise of new structures for organizing people and work. We believe that change is needed at all levels—individual, organizational, community, and global—and our publications address each of these levels.

We seek to create new lenses for understanding organizations, to legitimize topics that people care deeply about but that current business orthodoxy censors or considers secondary to bottom-line concerns, and to uncover new meaning, means, and ends for our work and work lives.

See next pages for other books from Berrett-Koehler Publishers

Patterns of High Performance
Discovering the Ways People Work Best

Jerry L. Fletcher

Discovering your individual High Performance Pattern—the distinctive sequence of steps you naturally follow when you are at your best-is the key to energized performance, heightened creativity, and consistent excellence. Jerry Fletcher shows how to discover your High Performance Pattern to sustain outstanding results in a variety of complex, real-life situations.

Paperback, 270 pages, 2/95 • ISBN 1-881052-70-2 CIP
Item #52702-356 $17.95

Hardcover, 9/93 • ISBN 1-881052-33-8 CIP
Item #52338-356 $27.95

301 Ways to Have Fun at Work

Dave Hemsath and Leslie Yerkes
Illustrated by Dan McQuillen

In this entertaining and comprehensive guide, Hemsath and Yerkes show readers how to have fun at work-everyday. Written for anyone who works in any type of organization, *301 Ways to Have Fun at Work* provides more than 300 ideas for creating a dynamic, fun-filled work environment.

Paperback, 300 pages, 6/97 • ISBN 1-57675-019-1 CIP
Item #50191-356 $14.95

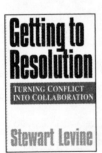

Getting to Resolution
Turning Conflict Into Collaboration

Stewart Levine

Stewart Levine gives readers an exciting new set of tools for resolving personal and business conflicts. Marriages run amuck, neighbors at odds with one another, business deals gone sour, and the pain and anger caused by corporate downsizing and layoffs are just a few of the conflicts he addresses.

Paperback, 240 pages • ISBN 1-57675-115-5 CIP
Item #51155-356 $16.95

Berrett-Koehler Publishers PO Box 565, Williston, VT 05495-9900
Call toll-free! **800-929-2929** 7 am-12 midnight

BK
Or fax your order to 802-864-7627
For fastest service order online: **www.bkconnection.com**

More books from Berrett-Koehler

Berrett-Koehler Publishers PO Box 565, Williston, VT 05495-9900
Call toll-free! **800-929-2929** 7 am-12 midnight

Or fax your order to 802-864-7627
For fastest service order online: **www.bkconnection.com**